Memoranda of Wishes

Vicki Ammundsen

Memoranda of Wishes

Wolters Kluwer

Vicki Ammundsen

CCH New Zealand Limited
PO BOX 33-270, Takapuna
Auckland 0740
Telephone: 0800 500 224
https://books.wolterskluwer.co.nz

About Wolters Kluwer

Wolters Kluwer enables legal, tax, finance and healthcare professionals to be more effective and efficient. We provide information, software, and services that deliver vital insights, intelligent tools, and the guidance of subject-matter experts.

We create value by combining information, deep expertise and technology to provide customers with solutions that improve their quality and effectiveness. Professionals turn to us when they need actionable information to better serve their clients.

Wolters Kluwer. When you have to be right.

Enquiries are welcome on 0800 500 224.

A catalogue record for this book is available from the National Library of New Zealand.

ISBN 978-1-77547-436-4

Published by CCH New Zealand Limited

First published 2022

Contents

Page

About the Author ... ix
Author's Acknowledgments ... x
Introduction to Memoranda of Wishes ... xi

1 Place of Memoranda of Wishes ... 1
- 1.1 Traditional role of settlor ... 1
- 1.2 Settlor cannot generally direct trustees ... 1
- 1.3 Alienation of property by settlor ... 2
- 1.4 Memorandum of wishes is mechanism to exert residual influence ... 2
- 1.5 Memoranda of wishes inform trustees ... 2
- 1.6 Trustees should rightly give weight to settlor's wishes ... 3
- 1.7 Memoranda of wishes are highly relevant consideration ... 4
- 1.8 Effect retention of settlor control can have on efficacy of trust ... 4

2 History and Development of Memoranda of Wishes ... 5
- 2.1 History of memoranda of wishes ... 5
- 2.2 Increase in use of discretionary trusts ... 7
- 2.3 Are memoranda of wishes trust documents? ... 9

3 Trustees' Reliance on Memoranda of Wishes ... 11
- 3.1 Trustees must make decisions in accordance with terms of trust ... 11
- 3.2 Trustees can be influenced by settlor's wishes ... 12
- 3.3 Language of judicial support for memoranda of wishes ... 12
- 3.4 Trustees must not blindly follow settlor's wishes ... 13
- 3.5 Trustees must act properly ... 13
- 3.6 Rejection of settlor's wishes ... 13
- 3.7 Memorandum of wishes does not negate fiduciary obligations owed by trustee ... 13
- 3.8 Trustees must act in interests of beneficiaries ... 14
- 3.9 Trustees must make their own decisions ... 14
- 3.10 Trustees must act reasonably ... 15
- 3.11 Trustees can decide not to follow settlor's wishes ... 15
- 3.12 Trustees must independently exercise their discretion ... 16
- 3.13 Balancing interests of different beneficiaries ... 16
- 3.14 Beneficiaries putting forward their own position ... 17

Page

3.15 Can trust terms be varied by memorandum of wishes? 21
3.16 Costs arising from improper consideration of memorandum of wishes 24

4 Disclosure of Memoranda of Wishes 27
4.1 Disclosing memoranda of wishes to beneficiaries 27
4.2 Disclosure following Trusts Act 2019 28
4.3 Disclosure in Erceg v Erceg 29
4.3.1 Background 29
4.3.2 High Court and Court of Appeal decisions 29
4.3.3 Supreme Court decision 30
4.4 Disclosure considered in light of interests of beneficiaries 30
4.5 Categorisation of memoranda of wishes 31
4.6 Context of request 32
4.7 Memoranda of wishes "rudimentary" 33
4.8 Trustees cannot resist disclosure due to "obligations of confidence" 33

5 Subsequent or Updated Memoranda of Wishes 35
5.1 Weight of earlier wishes compared with later wishes 35
5.2 Are settlors obliged to update memoranda of wishes? 36
5.3 Updating memoranda of wishes 37
5.4 Later wishes can supersede earlier wishes 38
5.5 Memoranda of wishes should be reviewed 40

6 Memoranda of Wishes as Core Documents 45
6.1 Core documents include any letter or memorandum of wishes 45
6.2 Presumption that trustees will give basic trust information on request 46
6.3 Trust information does not include reasons for trustees' decisions 47
6.4 Core documents are not necessarily trust information 47
6.5 Provision of basic trust information is subject to requirement that trustees have reference to procedure in s 53 48
6.6 Procedure for deciding whether presumption applies 49
6.7 Historic privacy considerations have not been included in Trusts Act 50
6.8 Memoranda of wishes and core documents 54

Page

7 Economic Settlors and Memoranda of Wishes 55
7.1 Wishes attributed to nominee settlors 55
7.2 Addressing true settlor 56
7.3 Nominee settlors have been long-term feature of trust landscape 56
7.4 Variations of trust if settlor is nominee 56

8 Memoranda of Wishes in Wills 57
8.1 Wishes and wills 57

9 Capacity Considerations 63
9.1 Capacity considerations 63
9.2 Fiduciary considerations 63
9.3 Capacity in context of memoranda of wishes 66
9.4 Capacity in a trust context generally 66
9.5 Clear ownership of wishes 67
9.6 Practical considerations of capacity 67

10 Drafting Memoranda of Wishes 69
10.1 Settlors can provide memorandum of wishes 69
10.2 Multiple trusts 69
10.3 Memorandum of wishes can provide an essential narrative 69
10.4 Matters to include in memorandum of wishes 75

11 Precedent Memoranda of Wishes 77
11.1 Memorandum of Wishes — Single Settlor 78
11.2 Memorandum of Wishes — Joint Settlors 83
11.3 Memorandum of Wishes — Economic Settlor 88
11.4 Memorandum of Wishes — Economic Settlors 93
11.5 Simple Memorandum of Wishes — Single Settlor 98
11.6 Simple Memorandum of Wishes — Two Settlors 102

Case Table 107
Index 111

About the Author

Vicki Ammundsen, BSc, BCom, LLB, TEP, is the founder and director of Vicki Ammundsen Trust Law Limited, a general practice law firm with a particular focus on wills, estates, trusts and law of equity. Vicki has extensive experience advising on all aspects of trusts and trust law.

Vicki has also acted as an independent expert on a range of trust, wills and estate issues and is a court-appointed estate administrator and trustee.

Vicki is a member of the ADLS Trusts Committee, a co-convener of the Trusts Special Interest Group (Chartered Accountants Australia New Zealand), a member of the Estate and Taxation Planning Council executive and the elected Chairperson of the global steering committee for the STEP Contentious Trust Disputes Special Interest Group.

Vicki is the author of a number of texts published by Wolters Kluwer CCH, including *Taxation of Trusts* (4th edition, CCH, Auckland, 2021), *A Practical Guide to Legal issues for Older People* (CCH, Auckland, 2021), *Trustee's Handbook* (5th edition, CCH, Auckland, 2020), *Trustee Liability: What Every Trustee Needs to Know* (CCH, Auckland, 2015) and the *Residential Care Subsidies Handbook* (CCH, Auckland, 2015).

Vicki has also presented the CCH Learning Trust Law annual webinar series for several years as well as speaking at conferences and providing professional education seminars and webinars for lawyers and accountants on a range of estate and trust law matters.

Vicki also publishes a well-regarded blog, Matters of Trust, which aims to provide useful and accessible information on trust law developments.

Author's Acknowledgments

In addition to acknowledging the assistance given by Wolters Kluwer CCH, I would like to acknowledge the assistance given by Hugh Ammundsen, Lee Treadaway and Reshma Korah and the parties involved in the different cases that guide and develop the law.

Vicki Ammundsen

Introduction to Memoranda of Wishes

The wishes of a trust's settlor or settlors must be considered by trustees as part of the exercise of discretion. However, the weight to be given to such wishes, and how these wishes should be recorded, is perhaps surprisingly controversial.

This guide to memoranda of wishes considers the development of memoranda of wishes, relevant case law and provides valuable guidance on how to construct a memorandum of wishes that will properly promote the settlor's intentions and directions to trustees.

This book also considers the legal position of memoranda of wishes with respect to the Trusts Act 2019 as core documents and in light of trustees' decision making and disclosure obligations.

Chapter 1
Place of Memoranda of Wishes

Traditional role of settlor 1.1
Settlor cannot generally direct trustees 1.2
Alienation of property by settlor 1.3
Memorandum of wishes is mechanism to exert residual influence 1.4
Memoranda of wishes inform trustees 1.5
Trustees should rightly give weight to settlor's wishes 1.6
Memoranda of wishes are highly relevant consideration 1.7
Effect retention of settlor control can have on efficacy of trust 1.8

1.1 Traditional role of settlor

The traditional role of the settlor (or settlors) of a family trust has been that of determining the terms of the trust and making the initial settlement onto the trust, to be held by the trustee or trustees for the beneficiaries alone. After this initial settlement, and any further settlements, the settlor (or settlors) can be expected to have a very limited role in the management of the trust.

1.2 Settlor cannot generally direct trustees

The settlor cannot expect to have rights either to direct the trustee's actions, or to take back the property the settlor has given away. This reflects the fundamental premise of a trust, whereby the settlor has lost control of assets that are settled onto the trust. See *Tarasiewicz v Titford* [2013] NZHC 3466; (2013) 3 NZTR ¶23-020.

This loss of control is an essential aspect of trust validity. See, for example, the decision of the Privy Council in *Webb v Webb* [2020] UKPC 22; (2020) 5 NZTR ¶30-011, which distinguished between a sham and the failure to make effective dispositions of property as follows at [87]:

> "There is, however, no inconsistency between the finding by Potter J, upheld by the Court of Appeal, that the trusts are not shams and a conclusion that Mr Webb's attempts to create the trusts have failed or are defeasible. Acceptance that Mr Webb intended to create trusts does not in any way preclude a finding that he reserved such broad powers to himself as settlor and beneficiary that he failed to make an effective disposition of the relevant property. Moreover, and as I have explained, the powers of clause 10 are conferred on Mr Webb as settlor, not in his

> capacity as Trustee or Consultant. These powers were therefore amply sufficient for Mr Webb to arrange matters in such a way that he alone would hold the trust property on trust for himself and no-one else, with the consequence that the legal and beneficial interest in all of that property would vest in him."

The conclusion of the Privy Council is recorded at [89] as follows:

> "... I will therefore confine myself to the substantive question whether Mr Webb's powers under each of the trust deeds were such that, in equity and in all of the circumstances of this case, he can be regarded as having had rights in the trust assets which were indistinguishable from ownership. In my view he plainly can. Mr Webb had the power at any time to secure the benefit of all of the trust property to himself and to do so regardless of the interests of the other beneficiaries. In my opinion, for the reasons set out at para 87 above, the Court of Appeal was plainly entitled to find as it did that the trust deeds failed to record an effective alienation by Mr Webb of any of the trust property. The bundle of rights which he retained is indistinguishable from ownership."

1.3 Alienation of property by settlor

It is important to appreciate the difference between the terms of a trust, which are such that any settlement onto a trust does not allow for the effective alienation of the property settled onto a trust, and a trust where the terms are such that any settlement comes under the control of the trustees but the settlor can provide additional guidance as to how the trustees should exercise that control.

1.4 Memorandum of wishes is mechanism to exert residual influence

The memorandum of wishes (also referred to as a letter of wishes, letter of guidance and similar) is therefore a mechanism by which the settlor can attempt to exert residual influence over the management of the assets the settlor has sacrificed control of. As noted in *Breakspear v Ackland* [2008] EWHC 220 (Ch); [2009] Ch 32:

> "The defining characteristic of a wish letter is that it contains material which the settlor desires that the trustees should take into account when exercising their (usually dispositive) discretionary powers."

1.5 Memoranda of wishes inform trustees

A memorandum of wishes informs trustees and may be considered persuasive with respect to the settlor's wishes and intentions. For this reason, a memorandum will generally be "legally significant," as it provides guidance for a trustee. While a memorandum of wishes must not be "blindly" followed and is a relevant consideration for trustees exercising their powers and discretions, the trustee must consider all other relevant matters. This is considered further at Chapter 3.

Some trust deeds will refer to memoranda of wishes and record whether a memorandum of wishes can be updated and who can provide one. More commonly, trust terms are silent on this point and the law regarding memorandum of wishes, which are recognised in multiple jurisdictions, has been largely developed through the common law.

1.6 Trustees should rightly give weight to settlor's wishes

The place of the memorandum of wishes was helpfully summarised in *Harrison v Harrison* [2015] NZHC 2935; (2015) 4 NZTR ¶25-029 at [53] where the High Court adopted the following summary from *Lewin on Trusts* (19th ed, Sweet & Maxwell, United Kingdom, 2014) at [29–162]–[29–163]:

> "***Settlor's wishes***
>
> . . .
>
> Trustees therefore rightly give great weight to the settlor's wishes, either expressed from time to time during his lifetime or recorded, usually in documentary form, before his death. Letters or memoranda of wishes from the settlor are now commonplace; on occasion a precatory clause is inserted in the trust instrument, for example asking the trustees to consider someone as the primary beneficiary. The significance of the settlor's wishes has grown with the growth of wide discretionary trusts and powers in preference to trusts comprising wholly or mainly fixed interests. Without some guidance from the settlor, trustees would often have difficulty in identifying who ought to benefit. 'The settlor's wishes', the Supreme Court [in *Pitt v Holt* [2013] UKSC 26; [2013] 2 WLR 1200] has held, 'are always a material consideration in the exercise of fiduciary discretions'. It was previously well established that the trustees are entitled to take serious account of the settlor's wishes and it is the better view that they are bound to do so; the notion that the trustees may be entitled to take it into account but not bound to do so is in our view wrong, for it is either a relevant consideration which in view of its importance ought to be taken into account or an irrelevant one which should not. The trustees may properly be led by the settlor's wishes to take a decision which they would not otherwise have taken. The propriety of deference to the settlor's wishes is also reflected in the decisions on applications by beneficiaries for disclosure of letters or memoranda of wishes. Although such applications have met with varying degrees of success, no criticism is made in them of trustees who

pay close attention to the settlor's wishes. In a different context, the court has treated it as a sufficient reason for overturning an appointment made by trustees that they believed that they were thereby giving effect to the settlor's wishes when in fact through a misunderstanding, they were not."

1.7 Memoranda of wishes are highly relevant consideration

Accordingly, the starting premise is that the terms of a memorandum of wishes are a highly relevant consideration for trustees before the exercise of any discretion afforded under a deed of trust.

1.8 Effect retention of settlor control can have on efficacy of trust

Can retention of too much settlor control be fatal to the efficacy of a trust either due to the value given to settlor powers or the inferences drawn as to the true effects of the trust?

It is necessary to balance permissible settlor direction with excessive settlor control such that the validity of the trust or the separation of the settlor and the trust can be challenged, as was the case in the decision in *Clayton v Clayton [Vaughan Road Property Trust]* [2016] NZSC 29; (2016) 4 NZTR ¶26-002. In that case, the amount of explicit control was such that Mr Clayton's powers were found to be property, the value of which was equal to the value of the assets of the relevant trust.

While memoranda of wishes are generally an avenue for expressing wishes, the extent to which such wishes and memoranda can be considered and adhered to by trustees is a rapidly developing area of law that requires vigilance and care.

The prudent settlor and where relevant, the adviser or trust administrator is wise to ensure that a settlor's memorandum of wishes is reviewed and updated when appropriate to do so; but at the same time careful consideration must be given both when advising as to what is appropriate in a memorandum of wishes, as well as when advising on the validity or weight to be given to earlier over later memoranda.

Chapter 2

History and Development of Memoranda of Wishes

History of memoranda of wishes 2.1
Increase in use of discretionary trusts 2.2
Are memoranda of wishes trust documents? 2.3

2.1 History of memoranda of wishes

The history of memoranda of wishes is perhaps surprisingly scant but can in large part be referenced to the increase in the use of discretionary trusts.

The following passages from *Breakspear v Ackland* [2008] EWHC 220 (Ch); [2009] Ch 32 at [6] to [8] provide a useful explanation of the genesis of memoranda of wishes.

> "6. The large increase in the use of wish letters has gone hand in hand with the rise in the popularity of discretionary trusts, in preference to the more detailed fixed interest trust. The combination of a broad discretionary trust accompanied by a wish letter may be said to have two particular advantages. The first, an advantage which it enjoys over the old-fashioned fixed interest trust, is that it preserves flexibility for the trustees in responding to changes in the beneficiaries' circumstances which are not or cannot be foreseen by the settlor. The second advantage, which stems from the placing of the trusts affecting the property and the settlor's non-binding wishes into separate documents, is that the settlor may make use of a confidential wish letter as the medium for the written expression of facts, beliefs, expectations, concerns and (occasionally) prejudices about the beneficiaries which it would or might be hurtful, impolitic or simply undesirable for him to include in a document which the beneficiaries had a right to inspect. That advantage may be summarised in the word confidentiality, so long as it is appreciated that the word has both a subjective and an objective connotation. Confidentiality may serve a purely selfish desire of the settlor to keep his wishes, beliefs and the communication of certain facts secret from the family. Objectively speaking, that secrecy may in many cases be thoroughly beneficial, since it may tend to preserve family harmony and mutual respect, while enabling trustees to be briefed as to matters relevant to the exercise of their discretionary powers, rather than kept in ignorance of them.

> 7. The use and advantages of wish letters in conjunction with broad discretionary trusts is not confined to family trusts. For example, the advantage of flexibility may be equally applicable to an employee trust. Nonetheless, the advantage of confidentiality is at its most obvious in relation to a family trust, and it is in the effect upon that advantage which any uncertainty or change in the law relating to disclosure of wish letters at the request of beneficiaries is at its most acute. Plainly, if the law is that, generally, wish letters are not disclosable, settlors will be encouraged to use them as the medium for the communication of valuable but confidential information relevant to the exercise of the trustees' discretionary powers. If by contrast wish letters are generally disclosable, that potential advantage is likely to be wholly closed off for the future, and the disclosure of genuinely confidential information in existing wish letters at the request of beneficiaries is likely to risk causing precisely the harm which led to that information being included in a wish letter in the first place, and to defeat what may to date have been real expectations of confidentiality in the minds both of settlors and trustees.
>
> 8. Since few would argue that clearly and rationally expressed wishes and relevant information included by settlors in wish letters could be treated by trustees as wholly irrelevant to the exercise of their discretionary powers, it is inescapable that their content will potentially be relevant, both to beneficiaries in monitoring the performance by trustees of their fiduciary obligations, and to the court in enforcing that performance where necessary and appropriate. Furthermore, the contents of a relevant wish letter may make all the difference to a beneficiary in understanding, in the context of an otherwise broadly drafted discretionary trust, what are or may be his or her expectations of benefit from the assets of a family settlement. While such expectations may on occasion be damaging, in particular to young beneficiaries, a broad knowledge of their prospects may be of significant advantage to them in planning both their own lives, and the education and maintenance of their children and other dependants. It is incidentally for this latter purpose that the claimants say that they have made their claim to disclosure."

This is confirmed in the following passage from *Lewin on Trusts* (19th ed, Sweet & Maxwell, United Kingdom, 2014) at [29-162]–[29-163]:

> "The significance of the settlor's wishes has grown with the growth of wide discretionary trusts and powers in preference to trusts comprising wholly or mainly fixed interests. Without some guidance from the settlor, trustees would often have difficulty in identifying who ought to benefit. 'The settlor's wishes', the Supreme Court has held, 'are always a material consideration in the exercise of fiduciary discretions'. It was

> previously well-established that the trustees are entitled to take serious account of the settlor's wishes and it is the better view that they are bound to do so; the notion that the trustees may be entitled to take it into account but not bound to do so is in our view wrong, for it is either a relevant consideration which in view of its importance ought to be taken into account or an irrelevant one which should not."

The role of the settlor to provide wishes is considered by the Court of Appeal in *Kain v Public Trust* [2021] NZCA 685; (2021) 5 NZTR ¶31-020 at [113] by reference to the orthodox role of the settlor as stated by Thomas and Hudson (Geraint Thomas and Alastair Hudson *The Law of Trusts* (2nd ed, Oxford University Press, Oxford, 2010) at [1.37]–[1.38]) who say:

> "The role of settlor is simply that of creator. Once creation has taken place, then there is no evident role for the settlor in the operation of the trust in his capacity as settlor . . . The settlor . . . drops from the picture absolutely and has no rights *qua* settlor, either to direct the trustees how to deal with the trust property or to reclaim the property which has been settled on trust."

The Court of Appeal's view as set out at [114] by reference to Thomas and Hudson is:

> "However, despite the absolute terms of that statement, the courts in all jurisdictions where trust law applies have in practice accepted that the settlor's wishes expressed independent of the provisions of the trust are a relevant consideration for trustees."

2.2 Increase in use of discretionary trusts

The seminal decision in *Schmidt v Rosewood Trust Ltd* [2003] UKPC 26 helpfully links memoranda of wishes in the context of the increase in the popularity of discretionary trusts. Also relevant is the drafting style of the time, where powers to add beneficiaries were not commonly used. Accordingly, a settlor needed a mechanism such as a memorandum of wishes to clarify the settlor's distilled and consider intentions (emphasis in [35] added):

> "34. Counsel have very properly referred the Board to a considerable number of authorities, some of them going back to the early years of the 19th century. It is appropriate to reflect that during the long period covered by these authorities (but especially during the second half of the 20th century) the forms and functions of settlements have changed to a degree which would have astonished Lord Eldon. By the 1930's high rates of personal taxation led some wealthy individuals to make settlements which enabled funds to be accumulated in the hands of overseas trustees or companies (see for instance *Vestey's Executor v IRC* (1949) 31 TC 1). This practice increased enormously with the introduction of capital gains tax in 1965. But increasingly stringent anti-

> avoidance measures encouraged legal advisers to devise forms of settlement under which the true intended beneficiaries were not clearly identified in the settlement. Indeed their interests or expectations were often barely perceptible. Rarely did a beneficiary take an indefeasibly vested interest with an ascertainable market value. Tax avoidance is therefore one element which has strongly influenced the forms of settlements; and once the offshore tax-avoidance industry has acquired standard forms its inclination is to use them, subject perhaps to some more or less skilful adaptation, even for clients whose aim is not to avoid United Kingdom taxation.
>
> 35. There is another element, also linked (though less directly) to taxation, which has encouraged the inclusion in settlements of very widely defined classes of beneficiaries. After the second world war estate duty was charged in the United Kingdom at very high rates, with much less generous reliefs for agricultural and business property than those now available. A wealthy landowner or businessman might be advised that the safest way to preserve his fortune was to give most of it away, while he was still in the prime of life, to trustees of an irrevocable settlement in discretionary form under which the settlor himself was not a beneficiary. It is not surprising that a settlor in such a position should wish to cover as comprehensively as he could all possible current and future claims on his bounty, since he was being asked to make an immediate, irrevocable disposition of much of his wealth, rather than being able to review from time to time the ambulatory dispositions in his will and codicils. But his lawyers might also advise him that the most natural expressions for defining discretionary objects of his bounty (such as 'relatives', 'old friends', 'dependants' or 'persons with moral claims') were of doubtful legal efficacy. So there was a tendency to define the class in the widest possible terms. The process can be seen in a long line of cases starting with *In re Gestetner Settlement* [1953] Ch 672. It led to *In re Manisty's Settlement* [1974] Ch 17, upholding the validity of an 'intermediate' power comparable to that in clause 3.3 of the Everest Trust (that is, a power to add as beneficiaries anyone in the world apart from a very small class of excluded persons)."

Given the large number of discretionary trusts in New Zealand, the importance of memoranda of wishes is self-evident. However, weight to be given to memoranda of wishes and the value of disclosure and related considerations need to be measured against the intrinsic value of memoranda of wishes. While in the context of trust information "more" might be equated to better, what the more is warrants reflection.

2.3 Are memoranda of wishes trust documents?

Memoranda of wishes can be seen as sitting outside the collection of documents that make up trust documents due to the fact that wishes are directed at trustees, but trustees are not party to a document recording the settlor's wishes. In "Theories of the Trust and What They Might Mean for Beneficiary Rights to Information" (2010) *New Zealand Law Review* 541–565, Jessica Palmer says:

> "C *Letters of wishes*
>
> The settlor's letter or memorandum of wishes is often seen as a special document, sitting just outside the collection of documents that make up the trust documents. Since disclosure should be based on accountability (whether that is understood to be an aspect of the court's inherent jurisdiction, as currently seems to be the case, or, as advocated here, an aspect of the fundamental nature of the trust and thus a right ascribed to the beneficiary), letters of wishes should accordingly be included in disclosure only if they are necessary to access in order to enforce the trustee's duties.
>
> It can be argued that where letters of wishes are understood to be non-binding expressions of expectation by the settlor, they do not confer any duties on the trustees, thus they do not confer any rights on the beneficiaries, and so should not rank as a trust document. No legal obligations have been imposed on a trustee to consider, let alone, obey a merely morally binding letter of wishes, and a trustee cannot be held accountable in respect of acting or refusing to act on the settlor's wishes. Likewise, if the letter is intended to be legally binding on the trustees, then accordingly it should be prima facie disclosable because it is in effect a trust document.
>
> On the other hand, it may be that this distinction between letters that are legally binding and letters that are only morally binding is somewhat overly clinical. As Briggs J said in *Breakspear*:
>
> > [F]ew would argue that clearly and rationally expressed wishes and relevant information included by settlors in wish letters could be treated by trustees as wholly irrelevant to the exercise of their discretionary powers[.]
>
> Accordingly, if a trustee, obliged to act in good faith, could not simply ignore the settlor's request, then perhaps the beneficiary should be entitled to see it. This may further be supported by consideration of the *Hastings-Bass* rule that allows courts to set aside trustees' decisions where those decisions were made in the absence of trustees taking into account relevant considerations that they ought to have taken into account. If the settlor's recorded wishes are relevant considerations, then the beneficiary ought to be entitled to access these to ensure they have been considered. An obvious weakness of this argument is that mere

> access to the settlor's wishes will not enable the beneficiary because, first, the trustees are not bound to act upon them and, secondly, the trustee's reasons for their decisions are normally not disclosed.
>
> Lee has suggested that the issue of whether letters of wishes should be disclosed ought to be determined by reference to the settlor's intention in using such letters. Letters of wishes are not for the benefit of beneficiaries (whose interest is in disclosure to give effect to trustee accountability), nor for the benefit of trustees (whose conflicting interest is in confidentiality to effect their autonomy), but rather are created for the benefit of the settlor to attempt to get the trustees to give effect to her intentions at a time when she no longer has significant ability to control, influence or require anything of the trustees. So the competing interests may not be just those of accountability and autonomy, but also of settlor intention.
>
> Given that the settlor has obviously chosen not to make her intentions, as expressed in the letter rather than in the trust deed, binding on the trustee, it could be said that she does not intend that they are necessary to the enforcement of the trust, and as such are not vital to the beneficiary's ability to hold the trustee personally accountable. Accordingly, even if the settlor's intention is considered relevant, letters of wishes generally ought not to be the subject of a beneficiary's right to access. The letter of wishes is not truly a trust document because it does not determine trustees' duties.
>
> However, it may be that such letters contain information that would indicate trustees' knowledge of circumstances relevant to beneficiaries, and thus relevant to whether the trustees are performing the trust honestly and in good faith. In this context, the role of the letter in disclosure would not be to determine the content of the trustees' duties because it cannot; but would be to provide evidence of whether the trustees' standards-based duties have been complied with. The question of disclosure in such a case could readily be determined by the court inspecting the letter first to assess its relevance to any such claim."

The importance of this analysis is to highlight the question as to whether a memorandum of wishes is in fact a trust document. Fundamentally, any document that expands on or relates to the terms of a trust is prima facie a trust document (and is a core document as that term is defined in s 45 of the Trusts Act). However, in the context of a settlor settling a trust and then essentially walking away or losing control, the residual value of a memorandum of wishes as either residual control or some other link to a trust settlement requires further consideration.

Moreover, given that the trustees must deal with the trust settlement on the terms as recorded, any residual control or influence must be considered in that light.

2.3

Chapter 3

Trustees' Reliance on Memoranda of Wishes

Trustees must make decisions in accordance with terms of trust 3.1
Trustees can be influenced by settlor's wishes 3.2
Language of judicial support for memoranda of wishes 3.3
Trustees must not blindly follow settlor's wishes 3.4
Trustees must act properly 3.5
Rejection of settlor's wishes 3.6
Memorandum of wishes does not negate fiduciary obligations owed by trustee 3.7
Trustees must act in interests of beneficiaries 3.8
Trustees must make their own decisions 3.9
Trustees must act reasonably 3.10
Trustees can decide not to follow settlor's wishes 3.11
Trustees must independently exercise their discretion 3.12
Balancing interests of different beneficiaries 3.13
Beneficiaries putting forward their own position 3.14
Can trust terms be varied by memorandum of wishes? 3.15
Costs arising from improper consideration of memorandum of wishes 3.16

3.1 Trustees must make decisions in accordance with terms of trust

Trustees must make their own decisions. In this regard, it is uncontroversial that a trustee must adhere to the terms of the relevant trust. This is now confirmed in the mandatory duties contained in the Trusts Act 2019, which provide at ss 23 and 24 that trustees have a:

> "**23 Duty to know terms of trust**
>
> A trustee must know the terms of the trust.
>
> **24 Duty to act in accordance with terms of trust**
>
> A trustee must act in accordance with the terms of the trust."

3.2 Trustees can be influenced by settlor's wishes

A decision influenced by a settlor's wishes is not necessarily a decision that is not the trustee's own decision. As noted in *Kain v Hutton (No 2)* (2004) 1 NZTR ¶14-022 at [301]:

> "... trustees must take serious account of the settlor's wishes but always appreciating that the ultimate decision is theirs. It follows that trustees may properly decide to act contrary to the settlor's wishes after taking account of all the relevant circumstances."

3.3 Language of judicial support for memoranda of wishes

The proposition put forward in *Kain v Hutton (No 2)* must now be considered in light of the somewhat stronger position put forward in the summary regarding memoranda of wishes in *Harrison v Harrison* (supra) and the later decision in *Public Trust v Kain* [2021] NZHC 1000; (2021) 5 NZTR ¶31-002, which considers the language of different judgments where the manner in which settlor's wishes have been expressed and can be followed or considered by trustees have been framed as:

- "It is perfectly proper for trustees to take a settlor's wishes into account" (*Kain v Hutton* [2007] NZCA 199; (2007) 2 NZTR ¶17-009 at [272])
- "... trustees are entitled to take [Settlor's wishes] into account" (*Chambers v SR Hamilton Corporate Trustee Ltd* [2017] NZCA 131; (2017) 4 NZTR ¶27-008)
- ".. a trustee may take into account the views of the settlor and of other beneficiaries as to the exercise of discretionary powers ... " (*Hartigan Nominees Pty Ltd v Rydge* (1992) 29 NSWLR 405)
- "[the] settlor's wishes are always a material consideration in the exercise of fiduciary discretions" (*Pitt v Holt* [2013] UKSC 26; [2013] 2 WLR 1200 at [66]).

In *Public Trust v Kain*, the court confirms at [123] that:

> "[123] A trustee is therefore obliged, as part of the exercise of its discretion, to have regard to a settlor's wishes for the purpose of making its independent assessment of the appropriate course of action. The trustee may ultimately decide to put those wishes to one side but in order to do so it must have had regard to the content of those wishes. They cannot be ignored and disregarded without the trustee having done so. It follows that a trustee is required to take into account the settlor's wishes."

As noted in *Chambers v SR Hamilton Corporate Trustee Ltd* (supra), "[i]t is necessary for trustees to read and understand a memorandum of guidance to discern the settlor's wishes, and then with those wishes in mind make an independent assessment of the appropriate course of action, taking into account not just the memoranda, but all relevant factors".

3.4 Trustees must not blindly follow settlor's wishes

A settlor's wishes are a material consideration. However, trustees must not follow them blindly (P Matthews, C Mitchell, Prof J Harris, Dr S Agnew *Underhill and Hayton Law of Trusts and Trustees* (20th ed, LexisNexis Butterworths, 2022) (Underhill & Hayton), 4.11). If the trustees were to follow the wishes of the settlor without turning their own minds to how their discretion should be exercised, any decision they made would not correctly be a decision of the trustees. However, trustees can be properly influenced by a settlor's wishes and can in fact make decisions "that the trustees would not otherwise have made, as long as trustees appreciate that the ultimate decision is theirs" (*Kain v Hutton* [2007] NZCA 199; (2007) 2 NZTR ¶17-009).

3.5 Trustees must act properly

Clearly a settlor's wishes are a relevant consideration. However, even if a trustee independently makes a decision in line with the settlor's wishes, it may be criticised on the grounds that it is otherwise unreasonable. See *Re the C Trust* [2012] JRC 086B, where a decision the trustees made was challenged because although arguably in line with the settlor's wishes as expressed, the court could see no support in the memorandum of wishes for the extreme position the trustees took that excluded the grandchildren from any possibility of benefit during the widow's lifetime.

3.6 Rejection of settlor's wishes

Trustees can reject the settlor's wishes if there is a proper basis to do so. In *Dever v Knobloch* [2009] NZHC 2013; (2009) 2 NZTR ¶19-042, the High Court held that rejection of the settlor's wishes "would require the trustees to be fixed with knowledge of, at the very least, a credible basis for challenging the approach reflected in the various memoranda of wishes ... " (at [61]). If the trustees take into account the settlor's memoranda of wishes, a trustee can still choose to act contrary to those wishes (*Bank of Nova Scotia v Borletta* (1994) 1 JIP 35).

3.7 Memorandum of wishes does not negate fiduciary obligations owed by trustee

Trustees owe fiduciary obligations to beneficiaries. If these obligations are not met, there are risks of actions from beneficiaries against trustees for breach of fiduciary duty. If a trustee simply complies with memoranda of wishes with no independent consideration, it would be difficult to support the proposition that the trustee has (unless this duty has been modified or excluded) independently exercised the trustees' duties and in particular the default duty now set out in s 32 of the Trusts Act that that a trustee has the duty to consider the exercise of power and that: "A trustee must consider actively and regularly whether the trustee should be exercising 1 or more of the trustee's powers."

The trustee must balance the wishes of the settlor with the fiduciary obligations owed under the trust. That said the decided cases clearly show that the courts will look at the trustee's exercise of discretion to ensure that the trustee exercises this in a responsible manner according to any expressed wishes (*Re Hay's Settlement Trusts* [1981] 3 All ER 786 (Ch D)) and may set aside trustee actions that are irrational, perverse or irrelevant to any sensible expectation held by a settlor (*Re Manisty's Settlement* [1973] 2 All ER 1203 (Ch D)).

3.8 Trustees must act in interests of beneficiaries

As a practical reality, following a memorandum of wishes may please some beneficiaries and failing to follow it may displease others. In this regard, it is helpful to reflect on the duty of impartiality in s 35 of the Trusts Act, which provides as follows:

> "**35 Duty of impartiality**
>
> (1) A trustee must act impartially in relation to the beneficiaries, and must not be unfairly partial to one beneficiary or group of beneficiaries to the detriment of the others.
>
> (2) This section does not require a trustee to treat all beneficiaries equally (but all beneficiaries must be treated in accordance with the terms of the trust)."

3.9 Trustees must make their own decisions

Fundamentally trustees must make their own decisions. This does not mean that a decision influenced by a settlor's wishes is not the trustee's own decision.

While a settlor's wishes have been held as always being a material consideration, trustees must not follow them blindly (Underhill & Hayton, 4.11). If the trustees were to follow the wishes of the settlor without turning their own minds to how their discretion should be exercised, any decision they made would not correctly be a decision of the trustees. However, trustees can be properly influenced by a settlor's wishes and can in fact make decisions "that the trustees would not otherwise have made, as long as trustees appreciate that the ultimate decision is theirs". See *Kain v Hutton* [2007] NZCA 199; (2007) 2 NZTR ¶17-009.

3.10 Trustees must act reasonably

Clearly a settlor's wishes are a relevant consideration. However, even if a trustee independently makes a decision in line with the settlor's wishes, it may be criticised on the grounds that it is otherwise unreasonable. See *Re the C Trust* [2012] JRC 086B, where a decision the trustees made was challenged because although arguably in line with the settlor's wishes as expressed, the court could see no support in the memorandum of wishes for the extreme position the trustees took that excluded the grandchildren from any possibility of benefit during the widow's lifetime. See 3.5.

3.11 Trustees can decide not to follow settlor's wishes

Trustees who take a settlor's memoranda of wishes into account can nevertheless choose to act contrary to such wishes. See *Bank of Nova Scotia v Borletta* (1994) 1 JIP 35. More commonly perhaps, trustees will consider a memorandum of wishes, but deviate to some extent based on the trustees' greater contemporary knowledge or of matters not known to the settlor at the time when the memorandum of wishes was drafted. This was the position in the Court of Appeal decision in *Chambers v SR Hamilton Corporate Trustee Ltd* [2017] NZCA 131; (2017) 4 NZTR ¶27-008, which states at [4]:

> "The last of the Memoranda shows that Mr White Senior wished each of his three children to enjoy the benefit of his estate equally and that the property be sold to one of his three children. We will return to the words of the Memoranda in due course."

By way of background to that case, the trustees could not follow the terms of memoranda of wishes because of facts not known to the settlor. The High Court directed as much adherence with the terms as possible. However, that was not the end of the matter and further consideration was given on the appeal decision as to whether trustees in doubt should exercise their own discretion or adhere completely to a memorandum of wishes. The Court of Appeal cited Lord Oliver in *Marley & Ors v Mutual Security Merchant Bank and Trust Co Ltd* [1991] All ER 198 (PC) at 201 who commented as follows:

> "A trustee who is in genuine doubt about the propriety of any contemplated course of action in the exercise of his fiduciary duties and discretions is always entitled to seek proper and professional advice and, if so advised, to protect his position by seeking the guidance of the court."

3.12 Trustees must independently exercise their discretion

Trustees must make their own decisions. However, this does not mean that a decision influenced by a settlor's wishes is not the trustee's own decision. As set out in *Kain v Hutton (No 2)* (supra) at [301]:

> "Trustees must take serious account of the settlor's wishes but always appreciating that the ultimate decision is theirs. It follows that trustees may properly decide to act contrary to the settlor's wishes after taking account of all the relevant circumstances."

This was expressed in *Chambers v SR Hamilton Corporate Trustee Ltd* (supra) as follows at [36]:

> "Settlors are entitled to express their wishes for the benefit of trustees, and trustees are entitled to take them into account. They can be important guidance to them in the exercise of discretionary powers. However trustees, whatever a settlor's wishes, must conscientiously apply their independent discretion in exercising their powers. Wishes can only be taken into account if they are not inconsistent with the purposes of the trust as appear from its written terms. Trustees should not blindly obey all settlor instructions. It is necessary for trustees to read and understand a memorandum of guidance to discern the settlor's wishes, and then with those wishes in mind make an independent assessment of the appropriate course of action, taking into account not just the memoranda, but all relevant factors."

3.13 Balancing interests of different beneficiaries

If the trustees were to follow the wishes of the settlor without turning their own minds as to how their discretion should be exercised, any decision they made would not correctly be a decision of the trustees. That said, trustees can be properly influenced by a settlor's wishes and can in fact make decisions "that the trustees would not otherwise have made, as long as trustees appreciate that the ultimate decision is theirs". See *Kain v Hutton* [2007] NZCA 199; (2007) 2 NZTR ¶17-009.

Importantly, trustees owe fiduciary obligations to beneficiaries. If these obligations are not met, there are risks of actions from beneficiaries against trustees for breach of fiduciary duty. If a trustee simply complies with memoranda of wishes with no independent thought, this might found an argument that the trustee has not independently exercised the trustees' duties. The trustee must balance the wishes of the settlor with the fiduciary obligations owed under the trust. That said, the decided cases clearly show that the courts will look at the trustee's exercise of discretion to ensure that the trustee exercises this in a responsible manner according to any expressed wishes (*Re Hay's Settlement Trusts* [1981] 3 All ER 786 (Ch D)) and may set aside trustee actions that are irrational, perverse or irrelevant to any sensible expectation held by a settlor (*Re Manisty's Settlement* [1973] 2 All ER 1203 (Ch D)).

This raises the practical reality that following the memorandum may displease some beneficiaries; while failing to follow it will displease others. This was considered at some length in *Re the Piedmont Trust and the Riviera Trust* [2021] JRC 248, which related to an application for directions with respect to the wind up of a trust where the beneficiaries were in different jurisdictions and would be taxed differently on the distributions made to them.

In this case, the terms of the memoranda of wishes favoured some beneficiaries over others and so, not surprisingly, there were differing views as to whether the trustees had paid sufficient regard to the memoranda of wishes (referred to in that case as letters of wishes). The following passages from that case are set out in full as they provide a useful contemporary assessment of memoranda of wishes from the context of a court considering whether trustees have made a proper assessment of these and other relevant considerations regarding the final disposition of the assets of a number of related trusts.

3.14 Beneficiaries putting forward their own position

In *Re the Piedmont Trust and the Riviera Trust,* competing beneficiaries took steps in the directions proceedings, which are discussed here. The starting premise was the view of some beneficiaries that the trustees had failed to adequately consider certain memoranda of wishes. The passages set out below from *Re the Piedmont Trust and the Riviera Trust* provide a helpful narrative setting out judicial consideration of memoranda of wishes in light of competing interests and viewpoints if there is clear evidence of family disharmony and the ebb and flow of favour with the relevant settlor.

The decision in this case is notable because although there are multiple trusts and also multiple memoranda of wishes, there is no "equivalence" between the settlors of each of the trusts and with respect to the generation of memoranda of wishes. This provides an aspect of realism with respect to the decision-making that confronts the trustees.

The background and relevant legal considerations are set out as follows:

> "62. As will be seen, one of the main submissions on behalf of the daughter and the daughter's child is that the Trustees have paid insufficient regard to the letters of wishes and in particular LOW 1, LOW 2 and the S Trust letter of wishes ('S Trust LOW'). Accordingly, we need

to remind ourselves of the part which letters of wishes should play in decisions by trustees.

63. In our judgment, the position can be summarised as follows:

(i) It has often been said in the past that trustees are entitled to take a settlor's wishes into account; see for example *Re Esteem Settlement* [2003] JLR 188 at [215]. However, the better view nowadays is that a settlor's wishes are a relevant consideration and trustees are therefore bound to take them into account pursuant to their duty to take relevant matters into account. As Lord Walker of Gestingthorpe said in *Pitt v Holt* [2013] 2 AC 108 at [66]: *'The settlor's wishes are always a material consideration in the exercise of fiduciary duties'*. See also *Investec Co-Trustees (Jersey) Limited v Kidd* [2012] JRC 066 at [63] and *Lewin on Trusts (20th Ed)* at 29-046.

(ii) However, a letter of wishes is not binding upon trustees. They must make up their own mind and are free to depart from the settlor's wishes. As this Court said in *Re Rabaiotti 1989 Settlement* [2000] JLR 173 at 189:

> *'The letter is, of course, not binding. If trustees slavishly follow a letter of wishes, their decision can be quashed on the grounds that it is not, in truth, the decision of the trustees. The trustees must make up their own minds as to how they should exercise their discretion in the best interests of one or more of the beneficiaries . . .'*

This observation is entirely consistent with the statement of Lord Walker in *Pitt v Holt* at [66] where, in a passage which immediately follows the sentence quoted at (i) above about the materiality of the settlor's wishes, he said:

> *'But if [the settlor's wishes] were to displace all independent judgment on the part of the trustees themselves . . . the decision-making process would be open to serious question.'*

(iii) The position is conveniently summarised by *Lewin* in the following terms at 29-049:

> *'Trustees, however, must form their own view when exercising their dispositive powers and must not unthinkingly act as ciphers for the settlor, whether alive or dead; to do so is a breach of trust and leaves their decision open to challenge.'''*

In this case, it was submitted that trustees can depart from a settlor's wishes where there is an objective basis to do so. This must be considered in light of *Chambers v SR Hamilton Corporate Trustee Ltd* (see ¶3.3) although in that case the consideration was not a focus on an objective basis for departure, but rather a more informed consideration of the relevant decision. In *Re the Piedmont Trust and the Riviera Trust*, the Court rejected the submission and instead confirmed at [63](iv) that "the settlor's wishes are always a material consideration" notwithstanding which ". . . trustees must make up their own minds".

Importantly in *Re the Piedmont Trust and the Riviera Trust*, the Court went on at [63](iv) to say that:

> ". . . None of the authorities or text books to which we have been referred mention the need for 'objectively justifiable grounds' and we do not think that it is a helpful expression; on the contrary, it is liable to lead to endless argument as to whether the trustees' reasons for departure are 'objectively justifiable'. If a settlor establishes a discretionary trust, he and the beneficiaries have to accept that, whilst his views will be a material consideration, the decision is now for the trustees. Provided that their decision is not outside the band of decisions which a reasonable trustee, properly instructed, could reach, the Court will, on the assumption that it is a momentous decision which is reached in good faith and is not vitiated by any actual or potential conflict of interest, approve the decision."

The weight that trustees place on a settlor's wishes should take into account any "unreasonable animus" against any particular beneficiary. See *GB Trustees Ltd v Stock* [2021] JRC 048 where Clyde-Smith, Commissioner said:

> "68. Whilst it is appropriate for G.B.Trustees to seek the views of John William Dick I as the economic settlor of the trusts (he is not a beneficiary), Advocate Preston agreed that an element of caution was required when considering his views about a member of the family with whom there had been a complete breakdown in their relationship with feelings running deep on both sides. Furthermore, they were currently engaged in litigation in the U.S. involving allegations of fraud and wrongdoing.
>
> 69. The wishes of a settlor are always a relevant consideration, but the trustee must guard against the possibility that a particular settlor's wishes are based upon an unreasonable animus against a particular beneficiary because if so, the trustee might conclude that little weight should be given to those wishes as against other factors. In the circumstances here, the wishes of John William Dick 1 as to Tanya Stock's exclusion had to be considered with caution."

Also relevant is the following passage from the judgment of the Court in *Re Rabaiotti 1989 Settlement* [2000] JLR 173; [2000] WTLR 953 in which the Court said at 190:

> "Circumstances will of course vary and the weight given to the letter of wishes will vary from case to case. Nevertheless, in general terms, the contents of the letter of wishes will undoubtedly form an important part

> of the trustees' consideration of the exercise of their powers. We are quite satisfied that a letter of wishes is a document which is closely related to the decision-making process and to the reasons for a decision, even where the trustees decide to depart from the letter. However, we disagree with Kirby, P in Hartigan (29 NSWLR at 419) that it is therefore a document which is to be treated as being ancillary to the trust deed. It is an informal document which the trustees are free to *ignore*. It is merely an expression of the settlor's wishes." [emphasis added]

Importantly, the passage above from *Rabaiotti* was addressing the issue as to whether a letter of wishes is to be treated as an instrument ancillary to the trust deed. This is an important consideration in the context of disclosure and what documents comprise the terms of a trust. For this reason, care is required to fully consider what is recorded in a formal trust deed, who has the primary carriage to draft this deed, and are there any ancillary considerations that are solely attributable to the settlor.

It is settled law that trustees are never free to fully ignore a letter of wishes, as any document that pertains to the circumstances of a settlement or the settlor's wishes carries a certain gravitas. However, as explored in *Re the Piedmont Trust and the Riviera Trust* trustees are free "to depart from" a letter of wishes (as differentiated from electing to ignore it).

When considering a letter of wishes, it is sensible to take the background of the different beneficiaries into account. This will be relevant (particularly if significant time has passed since a trust settlement) to determine the extent to which the trustees are required to exercise their own judgment and reasoning. In *Re the Piedmont Trust and the Riviera Trust*, the Court opined at [109] that:

> "109. We have carefully considered all the submissions from the parties. Although some trustees might have reached a different decision, we have come to the clear conclusion that the decision of the Trustees to make the Proposed Distributions should be approved, on the basis that it is a decision which reasonable trustees, properly instructed, could have reached. We would summarise our reasons for so concluding . . . ".

The message is not the reasons, but rather the process adopted to consider these by reference to the facts of the relevant case.

In any matter before the courts, a memorandum or letter of wishes will be relevant. As noted in *Re the Representation of Rysaffe Fiduciaires Sarl* [2021] JRC 230:

> "21. The Court paid close attention to the letters of wishes. Such documents are of course not binding on the Court or the Trustee but are something that a Trustee ought to have regard to in relation to a decision such as this, particularly where the assets of the Trust were donated by the Settlor and it is the Settlor and his family who were at all times the principal beneficiaries of the Trust.

> 22. Although not exhibited to the affidavits, the Court, at its request, was provided with copies of the letters of wishes executed by the Settlor in relation to the two Trusts. In the letter of wishes dated April 2009 in respect of the G 2000 Trust, the Settlor does not specify who he was referring to when he speaks of the Trust being held *'for the benefit of our children'* after the death of himself and his *'wife'* but in this context *'wife'* must mean F as this letter was executed after his marriage to F and, in the circumstances *'our children'* must, in view of the fact that M is F's only child, include reference to her as well as C, B and E. The letter of wishes indicated that subject to any provision made by the Settlor during his lifetime, then the children would receive one third of their respective share at age 25 years, the remaining two-thirds to be retained until they reach 35 years of age."

In that case, the Court went on to consider the very practical reality of the time frame of trusts and that there would be matters that would develop over time, of which a settlor could not have knowledge when the trust was settled:

> "23. As to the G 2008 Settlement, the memorandum of wishes was executed on an unknown date in 2008 (the Trustee's electronic system suggests 4th April 2008). This memorandum, expressed to be a *'guide'* to the Trustee from time to time of the Trust, said that the *Settlor's 'overall purpose in establishing the Trust'* was to have an arrangement in place which would provide financially for his family *'in a controlled manner'*. After his death he expressed the wish that the Trustee should *'add my children to the class of beneficiaries'* and *'after my death you should regard my children as the principal beneficiaries of the Trust. At present they are young and it is impossible to know their requirements or what their attitude to money will be'*. The Trustee was invited to use its discretion in dealing with them *'in the light of how they developed'*. Nonetheless, the Settlor expressed the wish (there are amendments to this particular clause made in the Settlor's hand) that the children receive all the income from the Trust once they had reached the age of 18 and if more than one then equally, with each child's notional share of the income accumulated until he or she had reached the age of 18 and added to the capital of the Trust. Whereas the letter of wishes for the G 2000 Trust indicated that the principal beneficiary after the Settlor's death should be his wife, there is no such indication given in respect of the memorandum of wishes for the G 2008 Settlement."

3.15 Can trust terms be varied by memorandum of wishes?

The considerations set out in respect of *Re the Piedmont Trust and the Riviera Trust* demonstrate the extent to which trustees must exercise their own independent decision making where guidance is incomplete. However, the corollary consideration is to reflect on how much trustees can depend on a memorandum of wishes to complement the terms of the relevant trust or trusts.

Importantly, trust terms cannot be read in light of a memorandum of wishes. This was confirmed in *Mackie Law Independent Trustee Ltd v Chaplow* [2017] NZHC 1570; (2017) 4 NZTR ¶27-025 where the settlor wrote a memorandum of wishes shortly before his death which included a direction that the settlor's partner was to live in the trust property for 3 months after his death (notwithstanding that she was not a beneficiary).

The memorandum of wishes in this case was drafted in the following terms:

> "2. As settlor of the Trust, I wish you to note my wishes. I may revise these from time to time. *I am aware that my wishes are not legally binding on you, but I expect that you will give these wishes careful consideration and implement.*
>
> . . .
>
> 4. I direct my trustees to allow QINGJUAN LU to remain in sole and exclusive occupation of whatever principal residence, we, or she is residing in as at the date of my death for a period not to exceed three (3) months from the date of my death.
>
> 5. Subject to the limited occupation right recorded herein to QINGJUAN LU, where I am survived by my daughter JOANNE she should receive priority.
>
> 6. *I direct my trustees to consult with Joanne Fleur Chaplow as the only living primary beneficiary of the Trust in relation to the property at 4/29 Sutherland Road, Point Chevalier (otherwise known as Henry Louis Court, Point Chevalier).*
>
> *In circumstances where JOANNE wishes for the property to be sold I direct my trustees to undertake the sale in an orderly fashion with the law firm of MACKIE & CO LIMITED to be appointed as the solicitor to act on the conveyancing transaction.*
>
> *I direct my trustees to apply the net proceeds to JOANNE in a tax-effective way and as to so protect against any claims which might ever be made against JOANNE's assets.*
>
> 7. *After I have died the Trustees should, following the sale of the Pt Chevalier property, consider whether the Trust should be wound up. I direct that instead of transferring any assets or capital of the Trust to my daughter JOANNE, those assets should be resettled for the benefit of JOANNE and her children in the discretionary family trust to be prepared by MACKIE & CO LIMITED.*

I direct that the structure of the Trust should be as follows:

(a) Sole settlor — Joanne Fleur Chaplow

(b) Initial trustees — Joanne Fleur Chaplow and Mackie Independent Trustee Limited

(c) Primary beneficiaries — Joanne's children

(d) Eligible beneficiaries — Joanne, Joanne's children and Joanne's bloodline relatives

I specifically record that the discretionary family trust shall not make provision for Joanne's husband.

In each case the trustees should confer with the beneficiary concerned to ascertain her wishes.

(emphasis added)".

As noted above, Ms Lu was not a beneficiary of the Trust. While the trustees were entitled to consider the memorandum as part of their decision-making process, they could only elect to adhere to the memorandum, provided that it did not conflict with the terms of the trust as set out in trust deed.

To the extent that the memorandum of wishes conflicted with the terms of the trust, the trustees were wrong to consider themselves bound to follow the memorandum. This reflects both the need for trustees to take an independent mind to any exercises of trustee powers and also to ensure that the trustees recognise and reflect on their duty to know the terms of the trust as set out in s 23 of the Trusts Act 2019 (A trustee must know the terms of the trust).

While this is largely self-evident, if a trust deed has been varied over time, or if a memorandum of wishes is utilised to remedy deficiencies in trust terms, trustees must carefully consider trust terms as varied and the extent to which any memorandum of wishes is expressing settlor wishes regarding the exercise of trustee powers, compared with the extent to which the settlor is rewriting trust terms. This distinction may sometimes be subtle, and care is required by trustees to identify the extent to which settlor wishes are just that.

If trustees fail to correctly appreciate the boundaries of memoranda of wishes, and as a result, act outside the terms of the trust, liability can follow.

In *Mackie Law Independent Trustee Ltd v Chaplow*, the primary beneficiary of the trust following the settlor's (Mr Munro's) death, was his daughter. Difficulties arose after Mr Munro's death over the trustees' adherence to the wishes, which included a direction that Mr Munro's partner be allowed to retain sole occupation of the trust property for 3 months after his death.

The memorandum of wishes also gave guidance regarding provision for Ms Chaplow. Relations between Ms Chaplow and the trustees deteriorated over the terms of a proposed resettlement and the trustees' fees. The background issue was the trustees' adherence to the memorandum of wishes. Although it was clear that the trustees were entitled to consider the memorandum of wishes as part of their decision-making process — and could elect to adhere to it — they could only do so provided that this did not conflict with the terms of the trust deed.

Further, the trustees were wrong to consider themselves bound to follow the memorandum of wishes (particularly if the wishes made directions that were not in accordance with the terms of the trust). The Court noted the frequent references to the memorandum of wishes in correspondence but that there were no minutes or resolutions other than one to follow the memorandum of wishes. It was also noted that there was no reference to the trust deed. This is a helpful reminder that not only should trustees bring independent minds to bare, but that if trustees fail to record any decision-making process, this can be evidence that there was no independent decision making.

The Court found that in adhering to the memorandum of wishes in the face of Ms Chaplow's express disagreement, the trustees were in breach of their obligations under the deed of trust.

3.16 Costs arising from improper consideration of memorandum of wishes

In *Mackie Law Independent Trustee Ltd v Chaplow*, it then became necessary to consider what the trustees' failings meant in the context of fees. This is because trustees can only be reimbursed for expenses that have been properly incurred. If fees charged are the subject of challenge, the onus lies on the trustees to demonstrate the extent to which fees are properly incurred.

A trustee may be honest and yet incur wholly unjustifiable fees. This can occur if trustees fail to appreciate where their loyalties ought to properly lie. See, for example, *Spencer v Spencer* [2013] NZCA 449; (2013) 3 NZTR ¶23-014. This can also occur when trustees incur excess costs due to a disproportionate level of caution. See *Re Chapman* (1985) 72 LT 67.

In *Mackie Law Independent Trustee Ltd v Chaplow*, the Court reviewed all the fees charged and found most not to be recoverable from the trust. As noted in this decision, the matter should have resulted in a straightforward resettlement.

While the trustees could seek to be indemnified for properly incurred expenses, they were not entitled to an indemnity for misunderstanding the extent to which they could not follow the memorandum of wishes, and also if they failed to follow appropriate guidance set out in the memorandum of wishes. As stated at [69]:

> "... The process was made far more difficult and expensive than it needed to be as a result of the trustees misunderstanding the terms of the memorandum of wishes and treating it as a binding document."

Chapter 4

Disclosure of Memoranda of Wishes

Disclosing memoranda of wishes to beneficiaries 4.1
Disclosure following Trusts Act 2019 ....4.2
Disclosure in Erceg v Erceg 4.3
Background 4.3.1
High Court and Court of Appeal decisions 4.3.2
Supreme Court decision 4.3.3
Disclosure considered in light of interests of beneficiaries 4.4
Categorisation of memoranda of wishes 4.5
Context of request 4.6
Memoranda of wishes "rudimentary" 4.7
Trustees cannot resist disclosure due to "obligations of confidence" 4.8

4.1 Disclosing memoranda of wishes to beneficiaries

Much contemporary case law around memoranda of wishes relates to whether memoranda of wishes can be disclosed to beneficiaries who want to view the document.

The privacy of memoranda of wishes may be justified where this is dictated by the relevant circumstances. The following passage from *Breakspear v Ackland* at [66] provides sage guidance:

> "Before applying those principles to the facts of the present case, I shall briefly summarise what I consider to be their practical effect in relation to family discretionary trusts, separately in relation to each of the three stages in which the issue may typically arise. First, trustees should in general regard a wish letter (that is a document from the settlor the sole or predominant purpose of which is or appears to be to assist them in the exercise of their discretionary powers) as invested with a confidentiality designed to be maintained, relaxed, or if necessary abandoned, as they judge best serves the interests of the beneficiaries and the due administration of the trust. This discretion to maintain, relax or abandon confidence arises regardless of a request for disclosure by a beneficiary, and persists regardless of the incapacity, death or **change** of heart on the part of the settlor."

However, requests for disclosure of memoranda of wishes must be reviewed in light of contemporary jurisprudence and what the position will be moving forward following the Trusts Act 2019 coming into full force and effect.

This chapter needs to be read in light of Chapter 6, which considers the effect of the inclusion of memoranda of wishes as core documents as that term is defined in the Trusts Act. This technical definition is important, not in the context of disclosure, but in the context of the relevance of core trust documents and how these are comprised.

4.2 Disclosure following Trusts Act 2019

Much contemporary case law around memoranda of wishes relates to whether the memoranda can be disclosed to beneficiaries who wish to review it.

The privacy of memoranda of wishes might be justifiable if the terms of the trust specify that any memorandum of wishes is to be kept confidential. This can also be consistent with the general position regarding the trustees' rights not to reveal reasons for decisions (see *Erceg v Erceg* [2017] NZSC 28; (2017) 4 NZTR ¶27-003) and the fact that a memorandum of wishes is commonly a letter addressed to the trustees, and therefore on the face of it private to the trustees (and not a trust document as such).

However, it is very important to review earlier decisions in light of the prevailing jurisprudence in the relevant jurisdiction.

The question as to disclosure of a memorandum (letter) of wishes is considered in the Jersey Royal Court decision regarding *Re Rabaiotti Settlement* [2000] JRC 90, where the Court states at [45] as follows:

> "... A letter of wishes will usually set out in some detail how the settlor would like the trustees to exercise their discretionary powers of distribution and, perhaps, of management of the trust fund. When trustees come to consider the exercise of a discretionary power, they will normally have the letter of wishes before them. The letter is of course not binding. If trustees slavishly follow a letter of wishes, their decision can be quashed, on the grounds that it is not, in truth, the decision of the trustees. The trustees must make up their own minds as to how they should exercise their discretion in the best interests of one or more of the beneficiaries. However, discussion is almost certain to involve references to the contents of the letter of wishes, such as whether the settlor's wishes remain appropriate; whether there are reasons to depart from his wishes; if so, what those reasons are and how they might impact on the wishes expressed by the settlor. Circumstances will, of course, vary and the weight given to the letter of wishes will vary from case to case. Nevertheless, in general terms, the contents of the letter of wishes will undoubtedly form an important part of the trustees' consideration of the exercise of their powers. We are quite satisfied that a letter of wishes is a

> document which is closely related to the decision-making process and to the reasons for a decision, even where the trustees decide to depart from the letter. However, we disagree with Kirby P in *Hartigan* that it is therefore a document which is to be treated as being ancillary to the trust deed. It is an informal document which the trustees are free to ignore. It is merely an expression of the settlor's wishes."

Historically, memoranda of wishes were private to trustees. This was revisited in *Erceg v Erceg* [2017] NZSC 28, which took the approach that disclosure of any trust information requested needed to be considered as an exercise of discretion by the trustees with no presumption for or against disclosure. It is useful to explore the decision in *Erceg v Erceg*, keeping in mind that the position has changed subsequently following the Trusts Act 2019 coming into full force and effect.

4.3 Disclosure in Erceg v Erceg

4.3.1 Background

In *Erceg v Erceg*, the relevant trusts were settled by the appellant's brother, the late Michael Erceg. The Acorn Foundation Trust was settled in 2004 and the Independent Group Trust was settled in 2002. Michael Erceg died in a helicopter crash in 2005. Shares in Independent Liquor (NZ) Limited (ILNZ), a successful business, were transferred to the trusts before Michael Erceg's death. Both trusts were wound up in December 2010. Ivan Erceg was neither a named beneficiary of either trust, nor did he receive distributions from either trust. He was, however, one of a class (among a number of classes) of discretionary and final beneficiaries of both trusts.

Ivan Erceg, the appellant, sought extensive disclosure, requesting that the trustees be required to provide 9 categories of documents. The request involved the inevitable disclosure of confidential information about the operation of the trusts, the business transactions they had entered, the identity of the beneficiaries, what beneficiaries had received by way of distributions from each trust and the trustees' reasons for decisions they had made.

The trustees refused his request after which, in September 2014, Mr Erceg began proceedings that were first heard in the High Court, which dismissed his claim. That decision was subsequently upheld by the Court of Appeal. Mr Erceg then appealed the Court of Appeal decision. The approved question in *Erceg v Erceg* [2016] NZSC 69 was: "Should the conclusion that disclosure not be made/required be set aside?"

4.3.2 High Court and Court of Appeal decisions

In the High Court, Courtney J dismissed Ivan Erceg's application on the basis that he did not having standing to bring the claim (see *Erceg v Erceg* [2015] NZHC 594; (2015) 4 NZTR ¶25-010). She found that Ivan Erceg's interest as a final beneficiary and his right to seek information in his capacity as a discretionary beneficiary were property for the purposes of the Insolvency Act 2006 and were vested in the Official Assignee on his bankruptcy. As the bankruptcy had not re-vested in the appellant, he did not have standing to bring the proceeding. However, she went to on express the view that if he did have standing, she would have exercised her discretion against requiring the trustees to provide copies of documents about the trusts to Ivan Erceg.

The Court of Appeal in *Erceg v Erceg* [2016] NZCA 7; (2016) 4 NZTR ¶26-001 dismissed Ivan Erceg's appeal, finding that Courtney J had been correct to exercise her discretion against ordering disclosure of any trust documents to Ivan Erceg, even though it reversed her finding that Ivan Erceg had no standing.

4.3.3 Supreme Court decision

The trustees of the trusts supported the decisions of the lower courts to withhold the trust documents. They sought to restore Courtney J's finding that Ivan Erceg had no standing to seek the orders requiring the trustees to provide copies of documents to him because of the effect of his earlier bankruptcy.

Ivan Erceg argued that the trust documents he requested should have been provided to him. He submitted that the lower courts were mistaken in overlooking the presumption that core trust documents should be disclosed to beneficiaries in the absence of exceptional circumstances.

The Supreme Court in *Erceg v Erceg* [2017] NZSC 28; (2017) 4 NZTR ¶27-003 extensively canvassed leading earlier authorities, including the Privy Council decision in *Schmidt v Rosewood Trust Ltd* [2003] UKPC 26 and the New Zealand High Court decision in *Foreman v Kingstone* (2003) 1 NZTR ¶13-018; [2004] 1 NZLR 841, which had set out a number of guidelines for trustee consideration when dealing with information requests.

4.4 Disclosure considered in light of interests of beneficiaries

The Supreme Court, in considering the appeal in *Erceg v Erceg* from the Court of Appeal, concluded that interests of the beneficiaries of the trusts in this case would best be met by declining to order any disclosure. The Court found that normally a primary discretionary beneficiary would have a good case for disclosure of the trust deed and financial statements relating to the trust. However, the unusual features of the *Erceg* case gave rise to real concerns about confidentiality, especially in relation to the identities of beneficiaries who had received distributions. The conduct of Ivan Erceg gave the Court reason for genuine concern about what he would do with trust information if he received it. The concerns outweighed the general expectation that basic trust information should be disclosed to a beneficiary.

At [56] of the judgment, the Supreme Court sets out guidance on the matters that need to be evaluated in relation to an application by a beneficiary for disclosure of trust documents. These include the nature of the documents sought (in particular, whether confidentiality issues arise, and whether the trustees will be required to reveal the reasons for decisions made by them in their disclosure); the reason for which the beneficiary seeks disclosure; the nature of the requesting beneficiary's interest; the likely impact of disclosure on the trustees, the other beneficiaries, the settlor and third parties; and whether measures can be taken to protect confidentiality of disclosed documents and to ensure they are used only for the purpose for which they were disclosed.

Helpfully the Supreme Court categorised the trust information required into 4 categories that have subsequently been widely adopted when considering requests for disclosure of trust information.

These categories are set out at [73] as:

(a) Category 1: Item 1 of the schedule (the trust deed and deeds of variation) and Item 6 (financial statements). These are basic documents for which the strongest case for disclosure can be made. Copies of these documents were provided to the legal advisers of the appellant's mother in *Erceg* 1.

(b) Category 2: Item 2 (minutes and resolutions). We see this category as similar to Category 1, save for the fact that disclosure without redactions may reveal the reasons of the trustees for the dispositions made by them.

(c) Category 3: Item 3 (documents relating to the dealings between the trusts and ILNZ), Item 4 (share valuations), Item 5 (gifting and debt documents), Item 7 (bank statements). These documents raise obvious issues of commercial confidentiality.

(d) Category 4: Items 8 and 9 (corporate documents of ILNZ). These are not really trust documents at all, though copies of the accounts were presumably held by the trustees when they were shareholders in ILNZ. It is hard to see why the trustees would hold the documents in Item 9, which could be expected to be held by the responsible executives of ILNZ under its new ownership.

4.5 Categorisation of memoranda of wishes

Although not referred to expressly in the "Erceg" categories, the settlor's memorandum of wishes had been requested. As stated at [56](a) of the Supreme Court case:

(a) *The documents that are sought.* Where a number of documents are sought, each document (or class of document) may need to be evaluated

4.5

> separately, given that different considerations may apply to basic documents such as the trust deed and more remote documents such as the settlor's memorandum of wishes.

Further as stated at [58]:

> "As mentioned earlier, the cases that were put to us in argument vary considerably in relation to the categories of documents sought. It can be misleading to see a case relating to a confidential memorandum of wishes, for example, as providing guidance in relation to a case involving a request for basic documents such as the trust deed and trust accounts."

4.6 Context of request

As was made clear in *Erceg v Erceg*, context where disclosure of trust information is requested is critical in the analysis of the trustee's decision making. Context can be considered in 2 ways, the first in light of the reason for the request and the other in light of the relationship of the beneficiary within the class of beneficiaries. For example, is the beneficiary one of a small class of contemporaries or a remote relative of the settlor for the request. While the requirement for a proprietary interest in a trust (eg as a final beneficiary) has been superseded by analyses relating to the due and proper administration of trust assets, some of the judicial reasoning that arose previously warrants being revisited in light of the contextual consideration. See, for example, the judgments of Kirby P and Sheller JA in the Court of Appeal of New South Wales in *Hartigan Nominees Pty Ltd v Rydge* (1992) 29 NSWLR 405 at 421 to 422:

> "I do not consider that it is imperative to determine whether that document is a 'trust document' (as I think it is) or whether the respondent, as a beneficiary, has a proprietary interest in it (as I am also inclined to think he does). Much of the law on the subject of access to documents has conventionally been expressed in terms of the 'proprietary interest' in the document of the party seeking access to it. Thus, it has been held that a cestui que trust has a 'proprietary right' to seek all documents relating to the trust: see *O'Rourke v Darbishire* (at 601, 603). This approach is unsatisfactory. Access should not be limited to documents in which a proprietary right may be established. Such rights may be *sufficient*; but they are not *necessary* to a right of access which the courts will enforce to uphold the cestui que trust's entitlement to a reasonable assurance of the manifest integrity of the administration of the trust by the trustees. I agree with Professor H A J Ford's comment, in his book (with Mr W A Lee) *Principles of the Law of Trusts*, 2nd ed (1990) Sydney, Law Book Co, at 425, that the equation of rights of inspection of trust documents with the beneficiaries' equitable rights of property in the trust assets 'gives rise to far more problems than it solves' (at 425):

'... The legal title and rights to possession are in the trustees: all the beneficiary has are equitable rights against the trustees. ... The beneficiary's rights to inspect trust documents are founded therefore not upon any equitable proprietary right which he or she may have in respect of those documents but upon the trustee's fiduciary duty to keep the beneficiary informed and to render accounts. It is the extent of that duty that is in issue. The equation of the right to inspect trust documents with the beneficiary's equitable proprietary rights gives rise to unnecessary and undesirable consequences. It results in the drawing of virtually incomprehensible distinctions between documents which are trust documents and those which are not; it casts doubts upon the rights of beneficiaries who cannot claim to have an equitable proprietary interest in the trust assets, such as the beneficiaries of discretionary trusts; and it may give trustees too great a degree of protection in the case of documents, artificially classified as not being trust documents, and beneficiaries too great a right to inspect the activities of trustees in the case of documents which are, equally artificially, classified as trust documents.'"

4.7 Memoranda of wishes "rudimentary"

Moving forward, while historically memoranda of wishes may have properly been classified as documents that are private between a settlor and trustees, these views may need to be reconsidered. As noted in *Jacomb v Jacomb* [2020] NZHC 1764; (2020) 5 NZTR ¶30-010 at [16]: "For example the financial information, and documents concerning the settlor's wishes, can be seen as documents that are rudimentary in order for a beneficiary to understand the nature of the Trust, and their interest in it".

4.8 Trustees cannot resist disclosure due to "obligations of confidence"

The case of *McGuire v Earl* [2020] NZHC 3083; (2020) 5 NZTR ¶30-025 and (Costs judgment) [2021] NZHC 129 — a successful application for trust information — considered the settlor's position regarding disclosure contained in his memorandum of wishes. Associate Judge Lester was not moved by the trustees' position that disclosure would breach their obligations of confidence stating at [37]:

"Assuming the Memoranda of Wishes does impose an obligation of confidence on the trustees, I do not consider that obligation sufficient to permit the trustees to resist the disclosure application. Firstly, in respect of the disclosure concerning the $181,996, given the wholly inadequate treatment of this in the financial accounts and the less than fulsome

> explanation set out at [22] above, full details as to where this money went and why, with all surrounding material, is at the heart of the trustees' disclosure obligations."

Disclosure was ordered with respect to all documents pertaining to distributions because of concerns regarding the accuracy of the financial statements. Disclosure was also ordered with respect to bank statements relating to all bank accounts.

Chapter 5

Subsequent or Updated Memoranda of Wishes

Weight of earlier wishes compared with later wishes 5.1
Are settlors obliged to update memoranda of wishes? 5.2
Updating memoranda of wishes 5.3
Later wishes can supersede earlier wishes 5.4
Memoranda of wishes should be reviewed 5.5

5.1 Weight of earlier wishes compared with later wishes

There is no absolute position regarding the weight of earlier versus later memoranda of wishes.

Some authorities suggest that a settlor's original intentions in setting up the trust should be given a weightier status than subsequent ones; other authorities refer to courts being unconcerned by series of memoranda of wishes (*Re E, L, O & R Trusts* [2010] WTLR 31). In *Breakspear v Ackland*, Briggs J leaves the question open.

However, *Re Collins Family Trust; Walker & Ors v Collins & Anor* [2009] NZHC 225; (2009) 2 NZTR ¶19-004 notes that arguments about a memorandum being superseded by events would carry more weight if the memorandum was signed before a particular event, suggesting that it is entirely appropriate for memorandum to be reviewed and amended from time to time as the settlor considers appropriate. In the Royal Court of Jersey *Re the C Trust* [2012] JRC 086B, the court appears to have the greatest regard to the settlor's final letter "reflecting his last and carefully considered wishes".

So, while it might be assumed that the only significant memorandum of wishes is one that is contemporaneous with the settlor's intentions when a trust is settled, given how long a trust can last, the author suggests that this is open to challenge considering the impossibility of foreseeing a future that may well involve beneficiaries not even born when the trust is settled.

Also, it can be argued that later memoranda should carry more weight given the significant professional encouragement to update a memorandum of wishes regularly, or "from time to time in the light of changing circumstances". Underhill & Hayton, at 4.15 cited in Trusts & Trustees, Vol 20, No 7, September 2014 at 718.

It may even be appropriate for a memorandum of wishes to be considered as "a living document" that can reflect changes in circumstance over time. There continues to be a tension between settlors losing control as a feature of trust validity, and memoranda of wishes that essentially attempt to exert residual control. Ultimately whether a memorandum of wishes is considered or followed is at the discretion of the trustee.

5.2 Are settlors obliged to update memoranda of wishes?

Abacus Trust Co (Isle of Man) v Barr [2003] EWHC 114; [2003] Ch 409 suggests that trustees have a positive obligation to consider the wishes of living settlors when exercising powers. This imputes a connotation of regular review.

Another aspect of memoranda of wishes, whether drafting new ones, or considering existing ones, is disclosure in light of the presumption of disclosure in the Trusts Act 2019 and the fact that a letter or memorandum of wishes is a core document for the purposes of the Trusts Act.

Management of disclosure can also be important. Careful consideration needs to be given to memoranda of wishes that are included in trust documents. However, a memorandum of wishes can be as much a shield as a sword. In *Carson v Lane* [2019] NZHC 3259; (2019) 5 NZTR ¶29-038, the memorandum of wishes played an important part in informing the Court about the settlor's wishes and satisfying the Court that relevant matters had been considered. As set out in that decision:

> "[115] As discussed, I do not accept the submission that the Trust was for the purpose of defeating the Children's claim. The Memorandum makes it clear the purpose is for members of Mr Carson's family and in addition the retention of assets to further research and development of Galloway cattle. Given the Trustees' obligations, it is inconceivable they would not take steps to locate the Children and provide for them in accordance with the Trust.
>
> [116] That said, I am not persuaded that the position is as clear cut as Mr Kelly would have it. In his submission, the appropriate provision for the Children is $1 million each and that is on the basis they remain discretionary beneficiaries under the Trust and therefore their interests will be provided for on an ongoing basis. That might be the case were the Trust's only purpose to provide for Mr Carson's family, but it is not. The Memorandum in particular stresses the importance of the farm properties and Galloway cattle. The first of Mr Carson's general wishes are that, as long as it is viable, the farm should continue with an emphasis on research and development. On the Trust's winding up, Mr Carson's preference is that the farm assets be transferred to Lincoln University. The Trustees are, of course, not bound to follow the

Memorandum but trustees will generally act in accordance with a memorandum, provided it is not inconsistent with the trust."

5.3 Updating memoranda of wishes

As noted above, some authorities suggest that a settlor's original intentions in setting up the trust should be given a weightier status than subsequent ones; other authorities refer to courts being unconcerned by a series of memoranda of wishes. See *Re E, L, O & R Trusts* [2010] WTLR 31. In *Breakspear v Ackland*, Briggs J leaves the question open. However, in *Re Collins Family Trust; Walker & Ors v Collins & Anor* [2009] NZHC 225; (2009) 2 NZTR ¶19-004, French J states that arguments about a memorandum being superseded by events would carry more weight if the memorandum was signed before a particular event, suggesting that it is entirely appropriate for memoranda generally to be reviewed and amended from time to time as the settlor considers appropriate.

In the decision of the Royal Court of Jersey *Re the C Trust* [2012] JRC 086B, the Court appears to have the greatest regard to the settlor's final letter "reflecting his last and carefully considered wishes".

The matter is helpfully addressed in *Public Trust v Kain* [2021] NZHC 1000; (2021) 5 NZTR ¶31-002. The current legal position is set out at [121] to [123] of this case as follows:

> "[121] I do not consider the language used by the Court of Appeal or the New South Wales Court of Appeal in *Hartigan* to be read as expressing a view that is inconsistent with the settlor's wishes being treated as a mandatory consideration by a trustee. Nor should those statements in the respective Court of Appeal judgments be viewed as being inconsistent with the United Kingdom Supreme Court's observation in *Pitt v Holt* that '[the] settlor's wishes are always a material consideration in the exercise of fiduciary discretions.' In both the *Kain* and *Chambers* decisions the Court of Appeal was commenting on the legitimacy of trustees taking into account a settlor's wishes rather than addressing the issue of whether doing so was mandatory or permissive. The statement in *Pitt v Holt* was adopted by this Court in *Harrison v Harrison* as part of Faire J's citation of the following passage from *Lewin on Trusts*:
>
>> The significance of the settlor's wishes has grown with the growth of wide discretionary trusts and powers in preference to trusts comprising wholly or mainly fixed interests. Without some guidance from the settlor, trustees would often have difficulty in identifying who ought to benefit. 'The settlor's wishes', the Supreme Court has held, 'are always a material consideration in the exercise of fiduciary discretions'. It was previously well-established that the trustees are entitled to take serious account of the settlor's wishes and it is the better view that they are bound to do so; the

> notion that the trustees may be entitled to take it into account but not bound to do so is in our view wrong, for it is either a relevant consideration which in view of its importance ought to be taken into account or an irrelevant one which should not.

[122] Notwithstanding a settlor's wishes, a trustee must conscientiously apply their independent discretion. A settlor's wishes can only be taken into account if they are not inconsistent with the purposes of the trust as appear from its written terms. Subject to that requirement, the settlor's expressed wishes can provide important guidance to the trustees when exercising their discretionary powers. However, the trustee must make an independent assessment of the appropriate course of action, taking into account not just the expression of wishes by the settlor but all material considerations. As the Court of Appeal observed in *Chambers v SR Hamilton Corporate Trustee Ltd*:

> Trustees should not blindly obey all settlor instructions. It is necessary for trustees to read and understand a memorandum of guidance to discern the settlor's wishes, and then with those wishes in mind make an independent assessment of the appropriate course of action, taking into account not just the memoranda, but all relevant factors.

[123] A trustee is therefore obliged, as part of the exercise of its discretion, to have regard to a settlor's wishes for the purpose of making its independent assessment of the appropriate course of action. The trustee may ultimately decide to put those wishes to one side but in order to do so it must have had regard to the content of those wishes. They cannot be ignored and disregarded without the trustee having done so. It follows that a trustee is required to take into account the settlor's wishes."

5.4 Later wishes can supersede earlier wishes

In *Public Trust v Kain*, Mander J considered the position where there are subsequent wishes that are inconsistent with earlier wishes. Context is a relevant consideration. As stated at [128]–[129]:

> "[128] As a starting point, which is no more than what the direction can be in the absence of any consideration of the disputed factual background, it appears plain that, all things being equal, subsequent statements of wishes by a settlor that are inconsistent with prior expressed wishes will supersede those earlier statements. That is the effect of the Court of Appeal's decision in *Chambers*. In that case, two memoranda of guidance were provided by the settlor that were issued some four years apart. An addendum that effectively revoked the substance of the second statement of wishes was issued some three

months later. The Court of Appeal identified the relevant expression of wishes to be used as guidance by the trustees in exercising their discretion were those extracted from the last memorandum, as amended by the addendum.

[129] *So long as they are consistent with the trust deed, there is a compelling logic for a trustee endeavouring at the time of exercising its discretion to view the most recent expression of wishes as being more relevant to its task than earlier inconsistent wishes.* Understanding a settlor's wishes at the time the trustee is exercising its discretion necessarily requires the trustee to take into account the most recent current guidance offered by the settlor. Whether that guidance is followed remains a matter for the trustee to weigh in the exercise of their discretion. In so doing, the trustee will have regard to whether those wishes are consistent with the terms of the trust's deed, and to all other relevant considerations, including the circumstances that applied at the time the settlor expressed their wishes."

[emphasis added]

The High Court then made the following directions with respect to the memoranda of guidance at [134]:

"(a) Public Trust is required to take into account the wishes and subsequent wishes of the settlor, Tom Couper, provided they are not inconsistent with the terms of the Trust and its purpose.

(b) Where subsequent wishes are inconsistent, Public Trust is in principle entitled to consider the most recent wishes as overriding earlier wishes. However, it remains a matter for Public Trust's assessment, in the exercise of its discretion to vest or make distributions, whether in the circumstances the subsequent wishes of the settlor, Tom Couper, should have that effect."

On appeal to the Court of Appeal (*Kain v Public Trust* [2021] NZCA 685; (2021) 5 NZTR ¶31-020), the direction at [134](a) was modified to make it clear that consideration of a memoranda of wishes is not mandatory. The Court of Appeal stated at [121] that:

"The wording used in the direction and how it is used in this context is important. 'Required to' imports an obligation. When read with 'take into account' it mandates they be taken into account. But that begs the question of what that taking into account requires the trustee to do. A requirement or obligation is different to an entitlement. An entitlement is a right which may or may not be exercised. In the present case Public Trust is entitled to take the wishes into account but it is ultimately for Public Trust to determine whether to act in accordance with the wishes. The

> current wording of the direction leaves some ambiguity about the nature of Public Trust's duty in this context."

The amended direction set out at [152] reads:

> "Public Trust is entitled to take into account the wishes and subsequent wishes of the settlor, Tom Couper, and to enable it to do so, it is necessary for Public Trust to read and understand those wishes. However, Public Trust can only take account of the wishes and subsequent wishes to the extent they are not inconsistent with the terms and purposes of the trust."

As at the time of writing, an application has been filed in the Supreme Court seeking leave to appeal the Court Appeal decision in *Kain v Public Trust.*

5.5 Memoranda of wishes should be reviewed

While many memoranda of wishes are pro forma documents prepared on general terms, a well-considered memorandum of wishes is an important aspect of trust governance that should not be overlooked and (subject to any subsequent judicial findings to the contrary that might follow the appeal in *Kain v Public Trust* [2021] NZCA 685; (2021) 5 NZTR ¶31-020) settlors may wish to review their wishes from time to time as circumstances dictate.

While the law may not be settled in this regard, at a practical level, if an updated memorandum of wishes is challenged, it is open to the court to determine to the matter. The general body of judicial view worldwide gives growing weight to subsequent memoranda of wishes.

The following passages from *Kain v Public Trust* are also instructive:

> "[137] We agree that no New Zealand case has yet been directly required to expressly consider the status of subsequent or inconsistent wishes.
>
> [138] However, both the *Chambers* and *Easton* cases dealt with wishes expressed after settlement and did not raise any particular issue about them.
>
> [139] The authors of *Lewin* state:
>
>> Moreover, trustees are entitled to have regard to the settlor's wishes expressed from time to time and are not confined to those expressed contemporaneously with the creation of the trust.
>
> [140] In support they cite *Chambers* and also *[In] Re R Trust* as cases which impliedly support that proposition. They also cite *Schmidt v Rosewood Trust Ltd* and *Re the Esteem Settlement* as examples of cases where the Court has expressly accepted reliance on subsequent wishes. In both cases the reference was passing. In *Schmidt*, the trust was established on 20 June 1995. In a letter of 31 October 1995, the settlor, who was also a beneficiary, expressed a wish to benefit his son in the

event of his death. The Court recognised that the letter provided clear evidence of his wishes and confirmed 'that the appellant may have a particularly strong claim on the trustees' discretion'.

[141] In *Re the Esteem Settlement*, the Royal Court of Jersey stated:

> [166] In our judgment, where the requests made of trustees are reasonable in the context of all the circumstances, it would be the exception rather than the rule for trustees to refuse such requests. Indeed, as Mr Journeaux accepted, one would expect to find that in the majority of trusts, there had not been a refusal by the trustees of a request by a settlor. This would no doubt be because, in the majority of cases, a settlor would be acting reasonably in the interests of himself and his family. This would particularly be so where there was a small close-knit family and where the settlor could be expected to be fully aware of what was in the interests of his family. Indeed, in almost all discretionary trusts, the settlor provides a letter of wishes which expresses informally his desires in relation to the administration of the settlement. Furthermore he may change his wishes from time to time. In our judgment it is perfectly clear that trustees are entitled (see *Abacus Trust Company (Isle of Man) Ltd v Barr* [2003] 1 All ER 763) to take account of such wishes as the settlor may from time to time express provided, of course, that the trustees are not in any way bound by them. The trustees must reach their own independent conclusion having taken account of such wishes.

[142] The statement 'Furthermore he may change his wishes from time to time' is not supported by reference to authority other than the case of *Abacus Trust Company (Isle of Man) Ltd v Barr*. In the *Abacus Trust Company* case the principal issue was the status of an appointment made in error.

[143] In this Court's decision in *Chambers* the issue of whether the trustee could take account of subsequent wishes was not directly in issue, but the Court did implicitly accept it would be proper for the trustees to have regard to subsequent wishes. In that case, following his wife's death the settlor had executed two statements of wishes intended to provide guidance to the trustees about how they should deal with the trust's assets after his death. The trust was settled on 7 November 2003 by Mr White Snr and his wife. The final beneficiaries of the trust were the Whites' three children. Mr White also executed a third document, an addendum to the second statement. The documents were dated 13 August 2006, 8 February 2010 and 10 May 2010. In the first statement Mr White proposed upon his death a current market value of the property be obtained and an offer made to all three beneficiaries or any one of them to purchase on the proposed basis. It was stated the children were

to be treated equally. In the second statement Mr White limited the option to purchase to Dr Chambers, the appellant, giving her an exclusive right to acquire the property on the basis of an up-to-date registered valuation. Only if she did not wish to exercise it would the property then be offered to the other two children. Again, it was stated the three children were to be treated equally.

[144] The addendum dated 10 May 2010 reverted in general terms to the original statement of wishes that all three children be given an option to purchase and it removed the preferential option for Dr Chambers only. The Court noted that even in the second statement, which provided for the right of Dr Chambers to purchase the property, the wish was expressed that all three children be treated equally. The Court then noted the preference for Dr Chambers was withdrawn in the addendum so that the two themes to be extracted from the last statement of wishes was that all be treated equally and also that, if possible, the property stay in the hands of the beneficiaries or one of them with no preference for Dr Chambers. Implicitly then this Court accepted that the trustees could take into account subsequent statements of wishes.

[145] In *Hartigan*, Mahoney JA accepted that subsequent wishes could be taken into account:

> There is, in my opinion, no distinction to be drawn between the views of a settlor expressed during the administration of the trust and those expressed before the constitution of it. Provided that the trustee is satisfied that views expressed before the constitution of the trust remain those of the settlor or would have been such, he may act upon or in accordance with those wishes.

[146] In principle there seems no reason why that should not be so. For example, a settlor of a trust who settles a farm into the trust may express a wish that the farm be retained within the family but then, as events and circumstances later change, might take the view that it was no longer appropriate or in the best interests of the family for the farm to be retained. The settlor could then change that particular wish so that the trustees would not have to consider that former wish when making decisions as to dispositions under the trust.

[147] We agree with Ms Anderson's point that it is relevant this is an unqualified discretionary trust. The fact that the trust deed provides for an equal distribution in default of the exercise of discretion to appoint income and capital is not, in some way, a dominant or overriding consideration. While the default provision of equality is a relevant consideration, it is no more than that. A statement of wishes that deviated from that purpose is not solely for that reason to be discarded or put to one side as inconsistent. We do however note that the passage

Ms Anderson cites from *Snell's Equity* to support the proposition appears to be derived from the case of *McPhail v Doulton*, a case quite different to the present. In that case the trust established a fund for the benefit of the staff of a company, their relatives and dependants, so it truly involved a large class of beneficiary. Of interest, in *McPhail* the Court observed:

> Equal division may be sensible and has been decreed, in cases of family trusts for a limited class, here there is life in the maxim 'equality is equity,' but the cases provide numerous examples where there has not been so, and a different type of execution has been ordered, appropriate to the circumstances.

As is often the case, context and the individual circumstances of the particular case will determine the appropriate outcome.

[148] We conclude that the Judge was correct to accept the status of subsequent wishes and that his direction at [134](b) accurately reflects the law."

[footnotes omitted]

As the core documents include any memorandum of wishes (see further in Chapter 6), it is recommended that all memoranda of wishes are retained whether revoked by a subsequent memorandum of wishes or not.

Chapter 6

Memoranda of Wishes as Core Documents

Core documents include any letter or memorandum of wishes 6.1
Presumption that trustees will give basic trust information on request 6.2
Trust information does not include reasons for trustees' decisions 6.3
Core documents are not necessarily trust information 6.4
Provision of basic trust information is subject to requirement that trustees have reference to procedure in s 53 ....6.5
Procedure for deciding whether presumption applies 6.6
Historic privacy considerations have not been included in Trusts Act 6.7
Memoranda of wishes and core documents 6.8

6.1 Core documents include any letter or memorandum of wishes

The Trusts Act 2019 has introduced a definition of core documents that must kept by trustees in subpart 3. This definition, which is set out below, includes "any letter or memorandum of wishes from the settlor".

> "Subpart 3 — Trustees' obligations to keep and give trust information
>
> *Documents to be kept by trustees*
>
> **45 Trustee must keep core documents**
>
> Each trustee of a trust must keep, so far as is reasonable, the following documents relating to the trust:
>
> (a) the trust deed and any other document that contains terms of the trust:
>
> (b) any variations made to the trust deed or trust:
>
> (c) records of the trust property that identify the assets, liabilities, income, and expenses of the trust and that are appropriate to the value and complexity of the trust property:

(d) any records of trustee decisions made during the trustee's trusteeship:

(e) any written contracts entered into during that trustee's trusteeship:

(f) any accounting records and financial statements prepared during that trustee's trusteeship:

(g) documents of appointment, removal, and discharge of trustees (including any court orders appointing or removing trustees):

(h) any letter or memorandum of wishes from the settlor:

(i) any other documents necessary for the administration of the trust:

(j) any documents referred to in paragraphs (a) to (i) that were kept by a former trustee during that person's trusteeship and passed on to the current trustee."

The Trusts Act provides that if there is more than one trustee, the obligation to retain core documents is met, provided that each trustee holds a copy of the trust deed and any deeds of variation, and provided at least one trustee holds the other documents and that those documents or copies of them will be made available to the other trustee or trustees on request. See s 46 of the Trusts Act.

If a trustee ceases to be the trustee of a trust, any trust documents held by the trustee at that time must be given to a replacement or continuing trustee.

Accordingly, if a trustee holds a memorandum of wishes, this must be retained by a trustee for the duration of the trustee's appointment as a trustee and must be passed on when the appointment as trustee ends.

However, safe storage of core documents is not the only trust information obligation.

6.2 Presumption that trustees will give basic trust information on request

The Trusts Act introduces a new presumption in s 51 that trustees will give basic trust information to every beneficiary. The basic trust information is:

"(3) The basic trust information is —

(a) the fact that a person is a beneficiary of the trust; and

(b) the name and contact details of the trustee; and

(c) the occurrence of, and details of, each appointment, removal, and retirement of a trustee as it occurs; and

(d) the right of the beneficiary to request a copy of the terms of the trust or trust information."

This information does not include any memorandum of wishes, but does refer to the right of beneficiaries to request trust information. In s 49, "trust information" is defined for the purposes of ss 50 to 55 as follows:

> "**trust information** —
>
> (a) means any information —
>
> (i) regarding the terms of the trust, the administration of the trust, or the trust property; and
>
> (ii) that it is reasonably necessary for the beneficiary to have to enable the trust to be enforced; but
>
> (b) does not include reasons for trustees' decisions."

6.3 Trust information does not include reasons for trustees' decisions

The core documents clearly comprise trust information and include trustee records of decisions. These decisions may include the extent to which any memorandum of wishes is considered. However, as trust information does not include reasons for trustees' decisions, care is required to separate trust information, for the purposes of disclosure, from the core documents.

6.4 Core documents are not necessarily trust information

The core documents clearly include documents that comprise trust information. That said, just because a document comes under the definition of a core document in the Trusts Act, this does not mean that the document is necessarily trust information. The Law Commission addressed this as follows in the Law Commission *Review of the Law of Trusts* (NZLC R130, 2013). Note that the reference to cl 33 should now be read as a reference to what became s 45 of the Trusts Act.

> "Commentary Clause 33 lists the essential documents that a trustee must retain in fulfilment of the trustee's duties. The provision makes this requirement clear for trustees. Clause 33 is not intended to imply any special status to the documents listed other than that they must be retained. In particular, this provision does not imply that a letter or memorandum of wishes is necessarily a trust document for any other purpose, including disclosure to beneficiaries. The use of the term 'so far as is reasonable' is intended to account for situations where it is unduly difficult to retain the documents, for instance where documents are

inadvertently lost or destroyed. It is also intended to imply that it may not be necessary for every low-level contract or account to be retained if such contracts and transactions are summarised in other documentation. Clauses 34 to 37 clarify details about the document retention obligation."

The reasoning set out above is expanded at 5.44 of the Review of the Law of Trusts as follows:

"Letters or memoranda of wishes

5.44 Letters or memoranda of wishes have been included in the list of documents that a trustee needs to retain because they are relevant documents that a trustee will usually have to consider when making decisions, particularly in relation to distribution. We recognise that the courts have found different memoranda or letters of wishes can have differing legal status depending on whether they are intended to be binding or not. We want to leave it open to the trustees (and the courts) to determine in the circumstances whether such a statement of the settlor's wishes is a part of the terms of the trust and its legal or moral effect. This recommendation is not intended to alter the law in this regard."

6.5 Provision of basic trust information is subject to requirement that trustees have reference to procedure in s 53

"52 Presumption that trustee must give information on request

(1) There is a presumption that a trustee must within a reasonable period of time give a beneficiary or the representative of a beneficiary the trust information that person has requested.

(2) However,—

(a) before giving the information, the trustee must consider the factors set out in section 53; and

(b) if the trustee reasonably considers (after taking into account those factors) that the information should not be given to the person,—

(i) the presumption does not apply; and

(ii) the trustee may decide to refuse the request for trust information."

6.6 Procedure for deciding whether presumption applies

The procedure for deciding whether the presumption applies is based on factors that have been developed over time in respect to information requests, as requests for trust information have segued from:

- information rights that are derived from identified proprietary interests (eg a beneficiary of a fixed trust or a beneficiary with a future contingent interest as a final beneficiary)

to

- information rights that reflect a beneficiary's right to the due and proper administration of a trust as an exercise of trustee discretion that are not founded in the need to demonstrate any proprietary interest and are an exercise of the trustees' discretion with no presumption either way

to

- following the introduction of the Trusts Act, a presumption that basic trust information will be given to every beneficiary, but that this presumption, and the corollary decision making if further trust information is requested is an exercise of discretion by refence in each case to the procedure in s 53 of the Trusts Act, which provides:

  "**53 Procedure for deciding whether presumption applies**

  The factors that the trustee must consider (for the purposes of sections 51(2)(a) and 52(2)(a)) are the following:

  (a) the nature of the interests in the trust held by the beneficiary and the other beneficiaries of the trust, including the degree and extent of the beneficiary's interest in the trust and the likelihood of the beneficiary receiving trust property in the future:

  (b) whether the information is subject to personal or commercial confidentiality:

  (c) the expectations and intentions of the settlor at the time of the creation of the trust (if known) as to whether the beneficiaries as a whole and the beneficiary in particular would be given information:

  (d) the age and circumstances of the beneficiary:

  (e) the age and circumstances of the other beneficiaries of the trust:

  (f) the effect on the beneficiary of giving the information:

  (g) the effect on the trustees, other beneficiaries of the trust, and third parties of giving the information:

(h) in the case of a family trust, the effect of giving the information on—

(i) relationships within the family:

(ii) the relationship between the trustees and some or all of the beneficiaries to the detriment of the beneficiaries as a whole:

(i) in a trust that has a large number of beneficiaries or unascertainable beneficiaries, the practicality of giving information to all beneficiaries or all members of a class of beneficiaries:

(j) the practicality of imposing restrictions and other safeguards on the use of the information (for example, by way of an undertaking, or restricting who may inspect the documents):

(k) the practicality of giving some or all of the information to the beneficiary in redacted form:

(l) if a beneficiary has requested information, the nature and context of the request:

(m) any other factor that the trustee reasonably considers is relevant to determining whether the presumption applies."

6.7 Historic privacy considerations have not been included in Trusts Act

The inclusion of memoranda of wishes as core documents, read in light of ss 52 and 53, means historic considerations of privacy between the settlor and trustee(s) are no longer necessarily valid (although these are reflected in the factor in s 53(c)). Significantly, given the inclusion of memoranda of wishes in core documents, there is arguably now a duty on trustees to request any memoranda of wishes as these are required to be held by trustees. Whether it is correct to equate this as a duty will be determined over time. However, the following excerpts from relevant cases show the progression of judicial views over time with respect to memoranda of wishes.

Re Beloved Wilke's Charity [1851] EWHC Ch J52 42 ER 330 confirmed the long-held proposition that trustees are not required to give reasons for the exercise of their discretion. The Court in that case recording that:

> "... Without occupying time by going into a lengthened examination of the decisions, the result of them appears to me so clear and reasonable, that it will be sufficient to state my conclusion in point of law to be, that in such cases as I have mentioned it is to the discretion of the trustees that the execution of the trust is confined, that discretion being exercised with an entire absence of indirect motive, with honesty of intention, and with a fair consideration of the subject. The duty of supervision on the part of this Court will thus be confined to the question of the honesty,

integrity, and fairness with which the deliberation has been conducted, and will not be extended to the accuracy of the conclusion arrived at, except in particular case. If, however, as stated by Lord Ellenborough in *The King v. The Archbishop of Canterbury* (15 East, 117), trustees thing fit to state a reason, and the reason is one which does not justify their conclusion, then the Court may say that they have acted by mistake and in error, and that it will correct their decision; but if, without entering into details, they simply state, as in many cases it would be most prudent and judicious for them to do, that they have met and considered and come to a conclusion, the Court has then no means of saying that they have failed in their duty, or to consider the accuracy of their conclusion . . . ".

Records of trustee decisions have continued to be considered matters that can resist disclosure. Naturally, over time, the approaches have become more nuanced. Historically, requests for disclosure required a property right to give the beneficiary standing to request information. A further relevant consideration flowing from the idea of property rights in trust documents was treating memoranda of wishes as the property of the trustees addressed in the memoranda. These ideas are fleshed out in *Re Londonderry's Settlement* [1964] EWCA Civ 6. Although memoranda of wishes were not considered, the ratio of that decision is clearly based in trustees' privacy in their decisions and the documents that related to these. As noted in that case:

". . . the trustees as trustees of the settlement are not bound to disclose to the defendant any of the following documents (that is to say)

(1) The agenda of the meetings of the trustees of the settlement,

(2) correspondence passing between the individuals for the time being holding office as trustees of or appointors under the settlement,

(3) correspondence passing between the said trustees and appointors or any of them on the one hand and the beneficiaries under the settlement on the other hand, and

(4) minutes of meetings of the trustees or appointors and other documents disclosing the deliberations of the trustees as to the manner in which they should exercise the discretionary powers conferred upon them by clause 2 of the settlement or disclosing the reasons for any particular exercise of such powers or the material upon which such reasons were or might have been based: provided always that the trustees are bound to disclose to the defendant at her request any written advice from their solicitors or counsel as to the manner in which the trustees are in law entitled to exercise such powers."

Schmidt v Rosewood Trust Ltd [2003] UKPC 26 — a seminal decision regarding the progression of disclosure — was an appeal to the Privy Council from the Isle of Man where one of the documents sought was a memorandum of wishes. This case focused on the exercise of discretion and the likelihood of benefit and did not expressly refer to memoranda of wishes as confidential, the Board concluding at 67 that:

> "67. However the recent cases also confirm (as had been stated as long ago as *In re Cowin* in 1886) that no beneficiary (and least of all a discretionary object) has any entitlement as of right to disclosure of anything which can plausibly be described as a trust document. Especially when there are issues as to personal or commercial confidentiality, the court may have to balance the competing interests of different beneficiaries, the trustees themselves, and third parties. Disclosure may have to be limited and safeguards may have to be put in place. Evaluation of the claims of a beneficiary (and especially of a discretionary object) may be an important part of the balancing exercise which the court has to perform on the materials placed before it. In many cases the court may have no difficulty in concluding that an applicant with no more than a theoretical possibility of benefit ought not to be granted any relief."

This was then followed and expanded in the context of New Zealand jurisprudence. As noted in *Foreman v Kingston* (2003) 1 NZTR ¶13-018 at [82]:

> ". . . A fundamental duty of trustees is to account to beneficiaries for the administration of the trust. There is nothing in the *Schmidt* decision that suggests a departure from that fundamental obligation. Indeed it would be an extreme result if in confirming the same rights of access to trust documents for beneficiaries with a transmissible interest and those with a discretionary interest or as objects of a mere power, a fundamental trustee obligation was in any way diminished or varied. To the contrary, the Privy Council endorses an approach to the issue based in fundamental principle."

Significantly the Court goes on to note at [83] that:

> "The Privy Council did not define or recognise a 'core category' of trust documentation to which beneficiaries have an absolute right of access. The Board preferred to leave the whole matter of disclosure within the discretion of the court in its supervisory jurisdiction."

When considering the extent of disclosure to be made, the obiter statement with respect to memoranda of wishes appears to clearly sever memoranda of wishes from "reasons for trustee decisions." See the following at [101]:

> *"l) Copies of all letters, memoranda of wishes or any other communications by the settlors of each of the JWF Foreman Trust, the MP Foreman Trust and the Foreman Family Trust to the trustees of those trusts.*

> The breadth of this category means that I am unable to determine it. It goes well beyond a request for disclosure of any 'memoranda of wishes' provided by a settlor to trustees. While I would incline to the view (without deciding the point), that memoranda of wishes or like communication from a settlor which exists outside the trust deeds are trust documents which should be disclosed to beneficiaries in the absence of a substantiated claim for confidentiality by the trustees (refer *Hartigan Nominees Pty Ltd v Ridge*), particularly when, as in this case, the trust deeds themselves include precatory provisions, the relief sought is in much broader terms. I decline the relief as sought. I have indicated my preliminary views in relation to any memoranda of wishes that may exist outside the terms of the trust deeds themselves. I invite the trustees to consider in the light of that indication whether there is any disclosure that should be made."

The next case of significance in this regard is *Erceg v Erceg* [2017] NZSC 28; (2017) 4 NZTR ¶27-003: see Chapter 4 at 4.2, 4.3.3, 4.4 and 4.5. In this case, a beneficiary of a trust that had been wound up made a far-reaching application for disclosure. The Supreme Court noted at [56] that the trust documents requested should be evaluated separately given that "... different considerations may apply to basic documents such as the trust deed and more remote documents such as the settlor's memorandum of wishes". Further, as noted in that case at [58]:

> "[58]As mentioned earlier, the cases that were put to us in argument vary considerably in relation to the categories of documents sought. It can be misleading to see a case relating to a confidential memorandum of wishes, for example, as providing guidance in relation to a case involving a request for basic documents such as the trust deed and trust accounts."

In *Erceg v Erceg*, the Supreme Court categorised the disclosure requested is divided into 4 categories as set out in 4.3. Perhaps surprisingly, memoranda of wishes are not referred to in any of the categories. We suggest that given the intrinsic nature of a memorandum of wishes, it would be a category 2 document, which is not a primary document, such as the trust deed, but closely related while being subject to confidentiality considerations.

In the case of *Jacomb v Jacomb* [2020] NZHC 1764; (2020) 5 NZTR ¶30-010, a pre-Trusts Act decision, the place of memoranda of wishes in the context of core documents is crystalised as follows at [16]:

> "[16] The third point is that the documents she seeks access to can properly be described as core trust documents. She has been provided with a copy of the Trust Deed, but she has not been provided with other basic information identified in [2] above — such as the Trust financial statements, trustee resolutions, memoranda of wishes or shareholder

resolutions related to the Trust. The further one goes down the list of materials sought in [2] above, the less fundamental the documents become, but they still all remain core documents related to the administration of the Trust. For example the financial information, and documents concerning the settlor's wishes, can be seen as documents that are rudimentary in order for a beneficiary to understand the nature of the Trust, and their interest in it."

6.8 Memoranda of wishes and core documents

Drawing the threads of this dialogue together, the chronology of cases referred to in this chapter demonstrate the elevation of memoranda of wishes to the ranks of core documents given the importance of the directional nature of memoranda of wishes but without obfuscating the need to consider and weigh the relevant confidentiality considerations.

Chapter 7

Economic Settlors and Memoranda of Wishes

Wishes attributed to nominee settlors 7.1
Addressing true settlor 7.2
Nominee settlors have been long-term feature of trust landscape 7.3
Variations of trust if settlor is nominee 7.4

7.1 Wishes attributed to nominee settlors

If the settlor is a nominee settlor, care is required to consider whether another person (the "true" or "economic" settlor) can give a memorandum of wishes. This issue was touched on, but not decided, in *Addleman v Lambie Trustee Ltd* [2017] NZHC 2054; (2017) 4 NZTR ¶27-016, which relates to "an unfortunate dispute between sisters as to what level of disclosure is appropriate for the affairs of the Lambie Trust (the Trust)".

As to the issue of who was the settlor of the trust, although the sisters' uncle was recorded as the nominal settlor, because he was the major shareholder and director of the company from which the initial assets came, it was very clear that he was not the true settlor.

It was argued that the concept of de facto settlors does not exist outside of the tax context. However, Woolford J who heard the matter determined that this was not an argument he needed to resolve.

It was noted that the uncle instead made clear that he effectively held his interests in the company as a bare trustee for the sisters' father, who had received the settlement on behalf of the one the sisters (Annette) and accordingly was the true settlor. The wishes that came to be central to the dispute were recorded in a letter to Annette's parents from Mr Kemp, their solicitor, who had met with and recorded Annette and her father's wishes.

Relevantly in this case, the "true" settlor is not clear. The point was considered but not decided. As noted in the decision at [9]:

> "... Counsel for Annette submits that Mr Palmer was only the nominal settlor of the Trust and that the de facto settlors of the Trust were in fact Mr Jamieson and Annette. Counsel for Prudence submits that the concept of de facto settlors does not apply outside of the tax context, and in any event is not borne out by the evidence here. This is not an argument I need to resolve in the present case."

Similar considerations apply when a trust is settled by parents or grandparents for a child or grandchild who although not a settlor is intended to be the person who can be looked to by the trustees for direction that might otherwise be provided by the named settlor.

7.2 Addressing true settlor

For the reasons set out above, it is sensible when drafting a trust deed to consider who should be able to provide a memorandum of wishes.

Similar considerations apply when a trust is settled by way of declaration of trust and there is no named settlor.

Given the long-term use of nominee settlors, it is perhaps surprising that memoranda of wishes drafted by a nominee have not been more definitively determined.

7.3 Nominee settlors have been long-term feature of trust landscape

Hartigan Nominees Pty Ltd v Rydge (1992) 29 NSWLR 405 was a case concerned with disclosure of a memorandum by a person who was in substance, but not nominally, the settlor. The terminology in that case as noted at 429 included a reference to the "instigator":

> "It is not uncommon for trustees holding property upon discretionary trusts to have from the settlor or instigator of the trust information as to his or her wishes as to how the discretionary powers are to be exercised. Trustees have, in such cases, taken into account the wishes of the settlor or instigator of the trust."

In that case, as with many others, nothing turned on this point. This does not mean that people who are not the named settlor cannot give a memorandum of wishes. However, it does mean that if the person providing the memorandum of wishes is not a settlor in a conventional sense, questions regarding the propriety of the person named in the memoranda of wishes directing the trustees can be questioned.

7.4 Variations of trust if settlor is nominee

If a Trust Deed does not name the true settlor, a practical consideration (if this is not set out in the deed of trust), presuming a suitable power of variation, is to amend the terms of the trust to specify who can provide a memorandum of wishes.

An appropriate clause to achieve this might be:

> [] has the right to provide the Trustees with a Memorandum of Wishes providing guidance to the Trustees that can be updated from time to time at []' s sole discretion.

Chapter 8
Memoranda of Wishes in Wills

Wishes and wills 8.1

8.1 Wishes and wills

A common feature of asset and estate planning in New Zealand is the use of wills to nominate a person or persons to exercise (most commonly) powers of appointment and removal of trustees, as provided for in the terms of the relevant trust. However, in some instances, wills and trusts and the relevant powers become entwined and at times trust powers and personally held powers can become confused and obfuscated.

These complications can be further exacerbated when family assets that might have been retained in personal ownership are disposes of to a trust. While memoranda of wishes have no obvious relationship here, what a settlor's wishes were, and how these wishes were shared in a family context, can warrant consideration.

In *Penson v Forbes* [2014] NZHC 2160; (2014) 3 NZTR ¶24-026, Ms Penson challenged a decision to remove her as a beneficiary of the S I Jack Family Trust settled by her mother Mrs Jack. Before her death, the trustees of the S I Jack Family Trust, who included Mrs Jack, removed Ms Penson as a beneficiary. Mrs Jack died soon after.

At the time of Mrs Jack's death, the trust in question owned her family home, which had been fully gifted.

Under the terms of the Trust, the trustees had the power to add to and vary the trust deed, to revoke trusts, powers or other provisions, discretions, alterations and variations. Express powers of amendment included the power to declare new beneficiaries and new classes of beneficiary.

The Court treated the power of removal as a fiduciary power, which, it was noted had constraints of exercise that go beyond fraud on the power and went on to say at [20] to [34] (references omitted):

> "[20] In *Equity and Trusts in New Zealand,* Dr Andrew Butler uses a number of descriptions which may be given to what I will call the duty to act rationally. He says:
>
>> A trustee must not exercise the trustee's discretions in a manner which is irrational, perverse, arbitrary or capricious. An exercise of a discretion in this way will be void.

And he adds:

> Often these flaws in the exercise of trustee discretions are dealt with under the head of *bad faith*. But it is better to deal with them separately because it is possible for a well meaning and honest trustee to act in these ways.

[21] One of the classic authorities in this area is the judgment of Templeman J (as he then was) in *Re Manisty's Settlement, Manisty v Manisty*, in which his Lordship observed:

> The court may ... be persuaded to intervene if the trustees act 'capriciously,' that is to say, act for reasons which I apprehend could be said to be irrational, perverse or irrelevant to any sensible expectation of the settlor; for example, if they chose a beneficiary by height or complexion or by the irrelevant fact that he was a resident of Greater London.

[22] I adopt, as conveying accurately the relevant concept of 'caprice', the Oxford English Dictionary definition of 'unaccountable change of mind'.

[23] Because Ms Penson initially filed an unparticularised statement of claim, she was subsequently required to particularise her allegations. She provided in the amended statement of claim the following particulars of the alleged breach in this regard:

(a) For some time prior to 3 August 2012 the deceased had taken a dislike to the plaintiff. The plaintiff gave no cause to the deceased for her dislike of the plaintiff.

(b) The deceased's dislike of the plaintiff was without justification and irrational.

(c) The decision to exclude the plaintiff as a beneficiary was made as a result of the deceased's personal dislike of the plaintiff. It was therefore in breach of the trustees' obligation not to put the interests of the deceased, as a trustee, ahead of the interests of the plaintiff as a beneficiary.

(d) The decision to exclude the plaintiff as a beneficiary was made without good cause and was therefore capricious and/or irrational.

(e) The decision to exclude the plaintiff as a beneficiary was made because of the deceased's personal dislike of the plaintiff and was made in bad faith.

[24] In his submissions for Ms Penson, Mr More dealt with the concepts of irrationality and good faith largely on a combined basis. To the extent that Mr More made submissions specifically towards irrationality or caprice, he stated:

> The plaintiff was a discretionary beneficiary, and before deciding to remove her, the trustees were under an obligation to consider that decision. They were not entitled to act capriciously. They were not entitled to take into account irrelevant considerations, such as the deceased's dislike of the plaintiff. The deceased put her own personal interests ahead of her obligation as a trustee. The trustees were required to consider the plaintiff's personal situation including her financial circumstances. There is no evidence that the trustees gave any consideration to the plaintiff's circumstances. See *Turner v Turner* [1984] 1 Ch 100.

[25] In relation to irrationality or caprice, Ms Penson's claim is therefore put upon the basis that the trustees in exercising their power to remove Ms Penson as a beneficiary acted in breach of trust because the decision was taken as a result of Mrs Jack's dislike of Ms Penson.

[26] Given that Ms Penson's assertion of breach of trust is in this regard put in that way, it is not tenable.

[27] To adopt Lord Templeman's terminology in *Re Manisty's Settlement*, the 'sensible expectations of the settlor' plainly include expectations that those who remain in her affections may remain in the class of discretionary beneficiaries and that those who fall from her affections may be removed from that class. The power to remove in this case is express and is not limited in its terms. There is no reason to read down the power in such a way as would exclude from the consideration of the settlor her intervening disaffection for her daughter. To again adopt the observations in *Re Manisty's Settlement*, the trustees' decision to exclude Ms Penson was not based on a capricious or irrational concept such as height or complexion. Rather, it was on Ms Penson's pleading based on the reason (or rationale) that one of the discretionary beneficiaries, who may have benefitted from this family trust, was no longer in the affection of her mother, the settlor of the family trust.

[28] The inability of the Court to invalidate the trustees' decision in the present circumstances is reinforced by the observation that the Court is not an appellate body for trustees' decisions. While particular Judges might have reached a different view if exercising the same discretion, that is insufficient. A Judge's view cannot be substituted for that of the trustees in whom the settlor imposed her trust.

[29] Towards the conclusion of the paragraph which I quoted from Mr More's submissions, he submitted that the trustees were in breach of trust by failing to consider Ms Penson's financial circumstances. Such a breach has not been separately pleaded but I will consider it under the heading of 'irrationality' as presented. It takes Ms Penson's case no further. The decision-making of the trustees in relation to the class of

beneficiaries is not alleged to have been taking place in the context of financial need. Rather, it is alleged to have been taking place because of disaffection. The financial circumstances of particular beneficiaries would have become a relevant consideration when distributions were made. The trustees were not at that point in August 2012.

[30] Ms Penson's allegation that the trustees, in making the decision to exclude Ms Penson as a beneficiary, acted in breach of their duty of good faith rested on the same five particulars as the irrationality pleading. Put in the negative, it is an allegation of bad faith.

[31] I adopt the description of that concept by O'Regan J in *Gailey v Gordon* where his Honour said:

> Bad faith in this context has been recognised as including a decision for an ulterior motive, taking into account of irrelevant considerations, and refusal to take into account relevant considerations and acting capriciously.

[32] The close relationship between bad faith and caprice understandably led counsel to rely on the same particulars for both pleadings.

[33] For similar reasons to those I have given in relation to the irrationality pleading, the bad faith pleading is untenable.

[34] Mr More addressed submissions to the bad faith pleading in this way:

> The deceased had taken a dislike to her daughter, and that was the reason for excluding the plaintiff as a beneficiary. It is quite clear from the trust deed, that Mrs Jack's intention was, that following her own death, the trust assets would be held for the benefit of her children and remoter issue. The exclusion of the plaintiff as a beneficiary was contrary to the purpose of the trust. Whilst as a mother, the late Mrs Jack might consider herself entitled to prefer her other children over the plaintiff, as a trustee she was not so entitled, without cause.

[35] There are at least two difficulties with Mr More's submission. First, it misstates or incorrectly assumes the intention of the settlor as expressed through the trust deed. The classes of beneficiary identified upon the establishment of the trust deed were simply the beneficiaries or the classes of beneficiary for the time-being. They cannot be read without reference to the right reserved to the trustees to add to, or exclude from, those beneficiaries or those classes. It is thus incorrect to suggest that the trust assets would be held for the benefit of Mrs Jack's children and remoter issue. The assets were to be held for the benefit of the beneficiaries as constituted from time to time."

Ms Penson claimed variously that the trustees acted in breach of trust in removing her as a beneficiary (breach of fiduciary duty, failure to act even handedly); and that the trustees had committed a fraud on a power.

The result was that Ms Penson's claim was struck out as having no prospect of success. The case, while not about memoranda of wishes, raises the risks of conflating testamentary and trust expectations.

If letters or memoranda of wishes are expressed in a will, the disclosure considerations of a core document before probate (as of course there may be a later will or the will could be invalid) means such practices warrant careful consideration. As reflected above, questions of settlor and testamentary capacity also arise. Consider the situation in which a memorandum of wishes is included in a will where the settlor lacks testamentary capacity but would otherwise have had sufficient capacity to draft a standalone memorandum of wishes or to update or amend an earlier memorandum of wishes.

For the reasons set out in this chapter, a memorandum or letter of wishes should generally be encompassed in a stand-alone document. Consideration on this point also highlights other documents confirming settlor intentions as were addressed in *Clement v Lucas* [2017] NZHC 3278; (2017) 4 NZTR ¶27-035. See 10.3.

A final consideration on this point is that assets can be settled onto or received by a trust at different times, and this draws further attention to the need to clearly signal the settlor's wishes by reference to the relevant trust assets.

Chapter 9
Capacity Considerations

Capacity considerations 9.1
Fiduciary considerations 9.2
Capacity in context of memoranda of wishes 9.3
Capacity in a trust context generally 9.4
Clear ownership of wishes 9.5
Practical considerations of capacity 9.6

9.1 Capacity considerations

Whether a settlor has the capacity to draft or update a memorandum of wishes is another relevant consideration.

There is no specific test with respect to capacity to enter a memorandum of wishes. If a person is amending (or drafting) a memorandum of wishes, as these reflect a settlor's personal wishes, and are not generally binding on trustees (*SR Hamilton Corporate Trustee Ltd v White* [2016] NZHC 1408; (2016) 4 NZTR ¶26-013), it is suggested that a slightly lower level of capacity may suffice. However, this has not yet been confirmed by the courts. Questions of duress and undue influence can be as relevant in the context of memoranda of wishes as to testamentary distributions. See *Green v Green* [2016] NZCA 486; (2016) 4 NZTR ¶26-021.

9.2 Fiduciary considerations

The fiduciary aspects of a memorandum of wishes also warrant consideration. While it may be attractive to argue that a settlor's wishes are personal and that there can be no fiduciary obligations, careful analysis of this proposition may be warranted particularly if these include dispositive instructions. The decision in *McLaren v McLaren* [2017] NZHC 161; (2017) 4 NZTR ¶27-004 usefully considers fiduciary obligations in the context of personally held powers of removal of beneficiaries. In that case, the appointor's argument was that his power of appointment was a general one vested in him personally, that it could not be constrained by any fiduciary obligations and that his position as appointor was to be considered distinctly from that as a trustee. In support of this, reference was made to the Court of Appeal decision in *Clayton v Clayton* [2015] NZCA 30; (2015) 4 NZTR ¶25-001, where the Court of Appeal stated that:

> "[104] Fiduciary obligations are not usually imposed by the courts on the exercise of a general power of appointment of this nature. This is because the courts recognise that a power of this nature is personal to the donee and may be exercised by the donee exclusively in his or her own interests. . . .".

The Court in *McLaren* distinguished the reasoning in *Clayton* on the basis that that decision related to a relationship property claim and a determination of the property right in powers. With respect to the close identity between the settlor and appointor (both being Mr Clayton in *Clayton*), the Court noted that:

> "[38] That analysis excluded the relationship between the equivalent of an appointor and beneficiaries from the categories of relationship recognised as having a fiduciary character. It is relevant to the reasoning in the *Clayton* judgments that the Principal Family Member (appointor) was also the settlor, and by analogy it would apply where there is a close identity between settlor and appointor. It leaves open the question whether respect for the unconstrained nature of a power vested in an appointor should also apply where there is no meaningful identity of interests between the settlor and the appointor. Further, that starting position does not exclude the prospect of factual circumstances arising in a particular relationship where circumstances of vulnerability of a beneficiary and the nature of the reliance placed on the appointor may justify the imposition of fiduciary obligations of an appropriate extent.
>
> [39] The basis for considering the imputation of fiduciary obligations in individual cases falling outside the relationships recognised as having a fiduciary character was put by the Supreme Court in *Chirnside v Fay* [[2006] NZSC 68; (2006) 8 NZBLC 101,831 at [80]] in the following terms:
>
>> 'It is clear from the authorities that relationships which are inherently fiduciary all possess the feature which justifies the imposition of fiduciary duties in a case which falls outside the traditional categories; all fiduciary relationships, whether inherent or particular, are marked by the entitlement (rendered in *Arklow* as a legitimate expectation) of one party to place trust and confidence in the other. That party is entitled to rely on the other party not to act in a way which is contrary to the first party's interests. . . .'"

Also see *Jay v Jay* [2014] NZCA 445; [2015] NZAR 861, where the Court of Appeal stated at [65] that ". . . no single formula or test has received universal acceptance in deciding whether a relationship outside the recognised categories has been established. The key feature in the imposition of a fiduciary duty is the entitlement of one party to place trust and confidence in the other . . . ".

In *McLaren v McLaren*, in providing a context to its reasoning, the Court considered both powers of appointment of trustees and beneficiaries to be fiduciary noting at [45] to [49] that:

> "[45] I note academic comment that is critical of reasoning to the effect that where a power to appoint or remove trustees arises in a personal capacity, that factor is determinative of whether it carries fiduciary obligations. Such comment cites Gilbert J's decision in *Carmine v Ritchie* for the proposition that fiduciary obligations will arise even if the position is held in a personal capacity.
>
> [46] Because of the critical importance of the identity of trustees, powers to remove or add them are distinguishable from powers to alter the class of beneficiaries. The former power naturally reflects a shared interest by all beneficiaries, whereas the latter is inevitably discriminatory between beneficiaries.
>
> [47] A relevant consideration to the nature of an appointor's power is the circumstances in which the trust was formed. The traditional form of family trust is where the settlor provides the majority of assets and the principal purpose of the trust is to provide the benefits of those assets for future generations. In that classic situation, an appointor is likely to be seen as standing in the shoes of the settlor which readily justifies the distinction between the personal nature of the powers granted to an appointor and the fiduciary nature of obligations owed by trustees.
>
> [48] In this case, the settlor had no interest at all in how the trust would be administered, so any on-going role for her (or her imputed interest in the trust's governance) was not in contemplation. Therefore there were no 'settlor's shoes' in which the appointor would be 'standing'. Bruce was the person who was likely to have the closest day-to-day involvement with the assets that were to be transferred to the trust, and to be involved with them for the longest period of time.
>
> [49] I reject the proposition that the characterisation of an appointor's powers as personal ones, rather than being derived from the status of a trustee, is determinative of itself. A relevant qualification is that if *Chirnside* considerations require the recognition of some fiduciary obligations in the particular circumstances that have arisen, then equity will recognise such obligations to the requisite extent. However, where the power is to alter the class of discretionary beneficiaries, the fact that such a power will inevitably be exercised discriminately as between beneficiaries puts a limit on the extent of any fiduciary obligations because it logically excludes any obligation to act even-handedly between all beneficiaries."

While *McLaren* related to the exercise of personally held powers of appointment, for the reasons set out, fiduciary considerations that might have application to powers of appointment cannot be entirely disregarded.

9.3 Capacity in context of memoranda of wishes

In light of the relevant fiduciary and similar considerations, the tests of testamentary capacity could be considered more relevant than the presumption of capacity in the Protection of Personal and Property Rights Act 1988.

The judgment of Cockburn CJ in *Banks v Goodfellow* (1870) LR 5 QB 549 remains the leading authority on testamentary capacity. The following statement from 567 of that judgment referring to *Harrison v Rowan* 3 Washington, 585 where the presiding judge succinctly observed the elements of testamentary capacity as follows:

> "As to the testator's capacity, he must, in the language of the law, have a sound and disposing mind and memory. In other words, he ought to be capable of making his will with an understanding of the nature of the business in which he is engaged, a recollection of the property he means to dispose of, of the persons who are the objects of his bounty, and the manner in which it is to be distributed between them. It is not necessary that he should view his will with the eye of a lawyer and comprehend its provisions in their legal form. It is sufficient if he has such a mind and memory as will enable him to understand the elements of which it is composed, and the disposition of his property in its simple forms . . . ".

9.4 Capacity in a trust context generally

The answer with respect to capacity in a trust context is not always entirely clear cut as evidenced by the Court of Appeal decision in *Green v Green* [2016] NZCA 486; (2016) 4 NZTR ¶26-021. This case concerned decisions that Hugh Green made following a diagnosis of cancer in 2010 relating to matters, including the appointment and removal of directors and trustees and the execution of a new will. Hugh Green's capacity to make these decisions and exercise the relevant powers was challenged. In a decision upheld by the Court of Appeal, the High Court found that Hugh Green was found to have capacity and to know and understand the effect of his actions. However, he was also found to have been subject to undue influence regarding decisions including entering into a new will. The decision in *Green v Green* also highlighted the need for independent advice for vulnerable clients. That said, *Green v Green* turns on its own unique facts, as do so many cases where capacity or exercise of powers are in issue. Care should be taken not to slavishly rely on judicial decisions, where common sense and fact sensitive analysis would be of more utility.

9.5 Clear ownership of wishes

If capacity or other matters relating to undue influence are relevant considerations, it is sensible to take steps to ensure the authenticity of recorded wishes and the genesis of the same. This will be more relevant when, for example, there is an updated memorandum of wishes that cannot be rationally reconciled with an earlier memorandum. This point was touched on, but not fully explored, in *Public Trust v Kain* [2021] NZHC 1000; (2021) 5 NZTR ¶31-002:

> "[132] Finally, and I mention the matter only briefly, the Kain siblings raised the issue of whether Tom Couper had been influenced by others in his statements of wishes. Questions were sought to be raised as to the authorship of some of the correspondence and statements of wishes. Details were canvassed of various examples that were said to illustrate that allegation. These are not matters that can be pursued in the context of an application for directions relating to issues of legal principle. The Kain siblings submitted that it would be inappropriate to place weight on statements of wishes where there are doubts about their authorship, particularly if the author stood to benefit from them. However, that is a matter for the trustee's consideration and does not bear on the legal principle put forward for my assessment."

This is discussed further at ¶10.1.

9.6 Practical considerations of capacity

While it is common for trust deeds to negate a settlor's power to appoint and remove trustees if the settlor is suffering from mental incapacity, it is rare for a trust deed to specify that a settlor cannot provide or update a memorandum of wishes if suffering from mental incapacity.

The Trusts Act 2019 does not provide clear guidance in this regard. In the context of trustees who can no longer perform the functions of a trustee, the Trusts Act provides the following at s 118:

> "(3) For the purposes of subsection (2), and without limiting that subsection, a person **loses the capacity to perform the functions of a trustee** if the person —
>
> (a) is subject to an order appointing a manager under section 31 of the Protection of Personal and Property Rights Act 1988; or
>
> (b) has a trustee corporation managing the person's property under section 32 or 33 of that Act."

However, there is no corollary provision regarding settlor's providing the trustees with a memorandum of wishes. Accordingly, it is prudent to retain evidence of capacity from a suitable authority (general practitioner who has cared for the settlor over time, psycho-geriatrician or older person practitioner as relevant) and retain this assessment with the memorandum of wishes. Also, where a capacity assessment is obtained for these purposes, it is important to properly inform the person carrying out the assessment. This will normally entail a letter setting out why the memorandum of wishes is being updated, the terms of the updated (and previous) memorandum of wishes and sufficient detail regarding the trust assets and family dynamics to appropriately inform the person assessing capacity.

9.6

Chapter 10

Drafting Memoranda of Wishes

Settlors can provide memorandum of wishes 10.1
Multiple trusts 10.2
Memorandum of wishes can provide an essential narrative 10.3
Matters to include in memorandum of wishes 10.4

10.1 Settlors can provide memorandum of wishes

A memorandum of wishes is usually drafted by the settlor or settlors whose wishes are being expressed. If professional assistance is provided, the wisdom of a memorandum of wishes being recorded on professional letterhead needs to be considered as this can obfuscate the nature of whose wishes are being expressed. This point was raised in *Public Trust v Kain* [2021] NZHC 1000; (2021) 5 NZTR ¶31-002 at [132], where questions were raised as to whether the settlor had been influenced by others.

Settlors may be prevented from creating a written record of their own wishes in certain circumstances — for example, when they have had a stroke which prevents or complicates preparing written advice — but they are fully competent to dictate their wishes. Where a settlor cannot complete a memorandum of wishes personally, the memorandum of wishes should include a reference to the circumstances, with the supporting evidence if relevant.

10.2 Multiple trusts

If a settlor is the settlor of more than one trust, it is not recommended that a single memorandum of wishes apply to each of the trusts. Even if each of the trusts has identical purposes and beneficiaries, given that trustees must exercise independent discretion, wide-ranging memoranda of wishes are not recommended. Consideration must also be given to the position if the trustees of each of the trusts change as well as to matters of confidentiality.

10.3 Memorandum of wishes can provide an essential narrative

The following discussion regarding the case of *Clement v Lucas* [2017] NZHC 3278; (2017) 4 NZTR ¶27-035 provides useful background as to how the proceedings could have been avoided with a suitable record of the settlors' wishes and is illustrative in the context of drafting effective memoranda of wishes for that reason.

Clement v Lucas concerns a family farming enterprise and illustrates the difficulties when beneficiaries cannot agree on how to give effect to the protections parents have put in place for the benefit of the beneficiaries. The contest at the heart of the matter was whether the trustees should distribute the trust assets equally between the 3 children who were the beneficiaries or in accordance with settlors' memorandum of wishes.

Key points that need to be taken into consideration include:

- the trust was settled to provide a mechanism to equalise interests between the settlors' children (to "even the ledger" – significant family assets having already been distributed to one son with smaller distributions being made to the other 2 children)
- the trustees took legal advice, which was later found to be incorrect
- during the hearing, although the trustees became aware of information that they were not previously aware of, the trustees' position remained that equal division of the trust assets was the best course of action
- the trustees declined to surrender their discretion to the court
- the deed was in standard form and did not contain any specific purposes
- the settlors made several memoranda of wishes
- it was important to the settlors that "each of the family should have a fair share"
- when new trustees were appointed, their review of the historical documents did not include pre-trust correspondence which amongst other things referenced the settlors' desire to "even the ledger"
- on 12 August 2016, the trustees wrote to the lawyers acting, "noting they had met with each of [the three children] and had heard their perspectives on the family history, the background to the acquisition of the Trust properties, the background to the creation of the Trust and the details of the issues that had 'brought about a collapse of the family relationship'. The letter stated:

  > Whilst unfortunate, we do not consider that it is our role to deal with or attempt to resolve the collapse of the family relationship, rather we consider our focus is to deal with the Trust's property in a manner that takes into account the best interests of the beneficiaries."

- On 3 October 2016, the trustees advised the beneficiaries lawyers that "[b]ecause it is impossible to reconcile the divergent opinions the trustees have agreed that in the first instance the properties should be sold on the open market, recording that this will not prevent the beneficiaries from participating in the purchase process, and then once the properties are sold the proceeds of sale will be distributed to the beneficiaries in a manner that it yet to be determined."

- On 19 October 2016, the trustees sought legal advice advising their adviser that:

  "We are concerned that consideration of matters pre-dating the creation of the trust would be a breach of our powers as Trustees under the Trust.

  The writer considers that consideration of such matters is not possible as the Trustees can only consider matters relating specifically to the affairs of the Trust. . . .

  We think in general terms that other than allowances for contributions for rates and similar made during the life of the trust that distribution should be made equally between the beneficiaries."

- On 25 October 2016, the trustees' lawyer advised that ". . . [i]n relation to the distribution approach I think that equality is best. I agree that the trustees cannot take into account things which happened outside of the trust."
- Orders were then sought by one of the beneficiaries under s 68 of the Trustee Act 1956.
- The trustees then sought orders under s 64 of the Trustee Act to sell the properties and divide the net proceeds amongst the beneficiaries equally.

A technical point raised at the hearing related to the need, when trustees are seeking directions under s 68 of the Trustee Act to establish, whether the power in question is concurrent between the deed and the Trustee Act. The following passages from the judgment provide useful guidance:

> "[68] There was no serious disagreement among counsel as to the scope of the Court's jurisdiction to intervene in the exercise of the Trustees' discretionary powers. Reference was made to the decision of the United Kingdom Supreme Court in *Pitt v Holt* where Lord Walker of Gestingthorpe, for the Court, considered and clarified the 'Rule in *Hastings-Bass*' — which for some years had been taken as authority for the proposition that:
>
>> . . . a trustee when exercising a power (for example) of appointment or advancement shall take into account all relevant considerations and refrain from taking into account any irrelevant consideration, and opens his decision to challenge if he fails to do as so required.
>
> [69] Counsel also referred to the decision of the High Court in *Masters v Stewart* where Mander J considered the application of *Pitt v Holt* in a case whose facts had some similarities to the present. As Mander J stated:
>
>> [28] The circumstances in which a Court will intervene in the exercise of a trustee's discretionary power are limited. Trustees, in

> the exercise of their fiduciary discretion, however, must act in good faith, responsibly and reasonably. The parameters of those obligations require greater definition.
>
> [29] Insofar as it is relevant to the present case, the parties are agreed that the Court will only set aside a trustee's decision if he or she has considered irrelevant considerations; failed to consider relevant considerations, or reached a decision that is perverse or capricious. . . .

[70] As Mander J went on to discuss, following the decision in *Pitt v Holt* there are important qualifications to these statements of principle. In the context of the present case, those qualifications are important.

[71] In *Pitt v Holt*, Lord Walker undertook a comprehensive review of the origins of the Rule in *Hastings-Bass* and the way the Rule had developed particularly in cases concerning trusts and tax-planning arrangements where, as Lord Walker noted:

> the arrangements have for one reason or another proved unexpectedly disadvantageous and, and the court has been asked to restore the status quo ante under the *Hastings-Bass* rule.

[72] It is apparent from Lord Walker's judgment, notably in his citing of academic criticism of the evolution of the rule in *Hastings-Bass*, that a key consideration in the Supreme Court's decision was to put limits on a rule that had enabled trustees to unwind transactions to which they had consented but which turned out to have unforeseen tax disadvantages. However, that was only one aspect of the Supreme Court's criticisms of a Rule the Supreme Court considered had started from a misinterpretation of the original *Hastings-Bass* decision. In its decision, the Supreme Court clearly intended to offer guidance applicable to challenges to trustee decisions generally and not just to those dealing with taxation issues.

[73] Drawing on the decision of Lightman J in *Abacus Trust Co (Isle of Man) v Barr*, Lord Walker approved or stated the following propositions about the circumstances in which the courts will intervene to set aside decisions of trustees said to have been made without regard to relevant considerations:

(a) As to whether a trustee's failure to consider relevant considerations must be fundamental:

> . . . the rule does not require that the relevant consideration unconsidered by the trustee should make a fundamental difference between the facts as perceived by the trustee and the facts as they should have been perceived. All that is required in this regard is that the unconsidered relevant considerations would or might have affected the trustee's decision.

(b) As to the relevance of the circumstances giving rise to the error by a trustee:

> What has to be established is that the trustee in making his decision has . . . failed to consider what he was under a duty to consider. If the trustee has in accordance with his duty identified the relevant considerations and used all proper care and diligence in obtaining the relevant information and advice relating to those considerations, the trustee can be in no breach of duty and its decision cannot be impugned merely because in fact that information turns out to be partial or incorrect.

In *Pitt v Holt*, Lord Walker said of the above statement by Lightman J:

> That is in my view a correct statement of the law, and an important step towards correcting the tendency of some of the earlier first instance decisions. If in exercising a fiduciary power trustees have been given, and have acted on, information or advice from an apparently trustworthy source, and what the trustees purport to do is within the scope of their power, the only direct remedy available (either to the trustees themselves, or to a disadvantaged beneficiary) must be based on mistake (there may be an indirect remedy in the form of a claim against one or more advisers for damages for breach of professional duties of care).

(c) If the rule applies, a trustee's decision is voidable:

> . . . Lightman J held that in cases where the rule applies . . . it makes the trustees' disposition voidable, not void. The Court of Appeal agreed with his analysis and so do I.

[74] I agree with the reasoning of the United Kingdom Supreme Court in *Pitt v Holt*. Given the absence of contrary authority from the New Zealand Supreme Court or Court of Appeal, I consider that its reasoning should be applied in New Zealand.

[75] The Supreme Court in *Pitt v Holt* did not consider whether unreasonableness constitutes a separate ground for intervention — in the sense that a court should be prepared to intervene if trustees reach a decision that the court concludes no reasonable trustee could rationally have reached in all the circumstances. As Mander J noted in *Masters v Stewart*, there have been different approaches on this issue in New Zealand High Court decisions. Following *Pitt v Holt* and the limits established by the United Kingdom Supreme Court for judicial intervention in trustee decisions, it would seem New Zealand courts should be slow to recognise unreasonableness as a separate ground for intervention if a trustee's decision is otherwise consistent with the trustee's duties and within the trustee's powers."

After discussing the relevant matters, the Court considered the questions to be decided.

The first question to decide – was it the settlors' wish that the trust be used to "even the ledger" among the siblings taking pre-trust distributions into account? The answer to this was yes. Coming to this conclusion, the Court referenced pre-trust correspondence and the memoranda of wishes. Accordingly, the legal advice that this could not be taken into consideration was wrong. As noted at [94]:

> "The Trustees acknowledged they did not have regard to the pre-Trust correspondence that explained Walter and Nola's intentions in setting up the Trust and which referred explicitly to the gifting of 160 acres to Keith, the wish to 'even the ledger' by making provision for the other two children, and to the intention to transfer 260 acres to Brian as well as the homestead to Keith. The Trustees cannot be faulted for not considering the correspondence because [the lawyer] had not brought it to their attention. Nonetheless, it was very relevant information, as the Trustees acknowledged in cross examination."

As noted by the Court at [98]:

> "There can be no doubt that the Trustees were under a duty to consider the purposes for which the Trust was established and the intentions of the Settlors even if, as Ms Robertson properly reminded me, the Trustees have a wide discretion in exercising their powers under the Trust Deed. As I have already held, the purposes of the Trust and the intentions of the Settlors included 'evening the ledger' among the siblings by having regard to earlier distributions. On its face, failing to have regard to such matters amounts to a breach of the Trustees' duty. However, following *Abacus Trust* and *Pitt v Holt*, that is not the end of the matter."

The difficulty for the trustees was that while the advice the trustees were given was wrong, the trustees had already communicated their intentions to the beneficiaries before this advice was given, and so could not be said to have relied on it.

The next consideration for the Court was whether to set the trustees' decision aside. As noted at [104] to [106]:

> "[104] I consider that the circumstances warrant setting aside the initial decision to sell the Trust properties and to direct the Trustees to reconsider both that decision and the decision in principle to distribute the net proceeds equally among the beneficiaries. The decision in principle was predicated on the first decision to sell, so cannot stand — notwithstanding [the legal] advice.

> [105] It is apparent from the correspondence that the Trustees looked at their initial task as essentially limited to three options: implement the Memorandum of Wishes, distribute the assets as proposed by Keith, or sell — although the Trustees said in evidence that there were sub-options within those options. The only one of the three main options reflective of the Trust's purpose was the first: implementation of the Memorandum of Wishes. But this was not favoured because of costs and, I infer, because it was opposed by Keith. Indeed, the Trustees' letter of 3 October 2016 says it was the inability to reconcile divergent opinions (presumably on the first and second options) that the Trustees went for the sale option — without acknowledging that Brian was 'implacably opposed' to this option.
>
> [106] I recognise the validity of the observation made by the Trustees in their letter of 12 August 2016 to the beneficiaries' lawyers that it was not their role to deal with or attempt to resolve the collapse of the family relationship. Equally, it was not their role to find a solution that all beneficiaries could accept. Rather, their role was to reach a distribution on the Trust assets having taken account of the Trust's purposes, which include 'evening the ledger' and, in that connection, taking account of earlier distributions — even if that produces a result with which one or more beneficiaries do not agree.
>
> [107] It is not obvious to me that if the Trustees approach the task in that light they will reach the same decision as the one they reached earlier. Having said that, I acknowledge . . . the Trustees have a wide discretion under the Trust Deed and it cannot be presumed that they would have made any different decision had they taken pre-Trust distributions into account. That, of course, is for the Trustees."

The result was that the trustees' decision to sell the trust's assets and divide these equally amongst the beneficiaries was set aside and the trustees were ordered to reconsider their decision. An appropriately drafted memorandum of wishes would have ensured that the trustees were adequately informed of the trust's purposes and the settlors' wishes.

10.4 Matters to include in memorandum of wishes

There is no prescription as to what matters should be canvassed or addressed in a memorandum of wishes. That said, matters to take into consideration when drafting a memorandum of wishes might include:

- guidance as to who should benefit from the trust
- the settlor or settlors' advice regarding the reasons for the creation of the trust

- whether assets owned personally or otherwise available to the beneficiaries are to be considered when the trustees are considering "needs"
- generational considerations such as who should benefit from a trust on the death of the settlor or the survivor of the settlors
- whether there is to be equality between children, grandchildren or remoter issue
- is recognition to be given to an individual's special circumstances and needs?
- is education to be a priority for children, grandchildren or remoter issue? And if so, what type of education would the settlors like to see preferred? For example, private as opposed to public and the option of tertiary and post-tertiary education and at what sort of institutes? Is assistance to be given to children to enable them to buy or build homes or provide support in careers or business activities?
- should the trustees consider distribution of capital, whether directly to beneficiaries or to related trusts for the benefit of a child and that child's issue
- to what extent should the trustees consult with any particular child to ascertain that child's wishes?
- provision for beneficiaries with special needs
- specific guidance relating to a beneficiary with drug, gambling or other addiction issues
- confidentiality considerations
- if the settlors do not want the existence of trust funds to negatively influence the beneficiaries' life choices.

Chapter 11
Precedent Memoranda of Wishes

Memorandum of Wishes — Single Settlor 11.1
Memorandum of Wishes — Joint Settlors 11.2
Memorandum of Wishes — Economic Settlor 11.3
Memorandum of Wishes — Economic Settlors 11.4
Simple Memorandum of Wishes — Single Settlor 11.5
Simple Memorandum of Wishes — Two Settlors 11.6

Precedents can be used to guide the generation of memoranda of wishes. The following precedents are necessarily general and are designed to be adapted and significantly amended to address individual circumstances. It is preferable that a settlor or settlors record their considered wishes in their own words. That said, it is recognised that, for some settlors, the "blank page" is so intimidating that it prevents an accurate record of wishes. If this is the case, the simple precedent options may provide a more accessible starting point to record memoranda of wishes.

The most important aspect of these precedents is to allow a forum for settlors to record their genuine wishes with respect to why a trust has been settled, how they want generations of family to benefit from the trust and to provide meaningful guidance to trustees.

While the Court of Appeal decision in *Kain v Public Trust* [2021] NZCA 685; (2021) 5 NZTR ¶31-020 has expressly permitted trustees to take subsequent memoranda of wishes into account, it cannot be presumed that settlors will have a further opportunity to update their wishes. Circumstances outside the current legal paradigm, such as a loss of capacity or untimely death, could remove the chance to "correct" or amend a memorandum of wishes.

The attached memoranda of wishes include guidance notes for the settlor or settlor and their advisers.

Precedents attached are:

1. Memorandum of wishes — single settlor
2. Memorandum of wishes — joint settlors
3. Memorandum of wishes — economic settlor
4. Memorandum of wishes — economic settlors
5. Simple memorandum of wishes — single settlor
6. Simple memorandum of wishes — two settlors.

11.1 Memorandum of Wishes — Single Settlor

Notes to the settlor regarding drafting a memorandum of wishes

This memorandum of wishes is in draft, for your consideration. We have prepared this memorandum based on our discussion with you. Please amend this document to reflect your wishes. Please include anything that you think is important to you about the purpose of the trust in this memorandum of wishes, even if you are unsure whether it is relevant. We can discuss any points we feel should not be included.

In considering the terms or form of your memorandum of wishes, it is important to consider why the Trust was settled, and what you intend the Trust to achieve.

Please note that this memorandum of wishes will not be binding on the Trustees, but it is highly persuasive and intended to provide guidance for the Trustees in the event you are unable to tell the Trustees what you wish them to do during your lifetime, and also after your death. Accordingly, your memorandum of wishes should be drafted following careful consideration regarding the Trust's purposes. As stated by the Court of Appeal in *Chambers v SR Hamilton Corporate Trustee Ltd* [2017] NZCA 131; (2017) 4 NZTR ¶27-008 at [36]:

> "Settlors are entitled to express their wishes for the benefit of trustees, and trustees are entitled to take them into account. They can be important guidance to them in the exercise of discretionary powers. However trustees, whatever a settlor's wishes, must conscientiously apply their independent discretion in exercising their powers. Wishes can only be taken into account if they are not inconsistent with the purposes of the trust as appear from its written terms. Trustees should not blindly obey all settlor instructions. It is necessary for trustees to read and understand a memorandum of guidance to discern the settlor's wishes, and then with those wishes in mind make an independent assessment of the appropriate course of action, taking into account not just the memoranda, but all relevant factors."

In *Pitt v Holt* [2013] 2 WLR 1200, the United Kingdom Supreme Court also reflects on the extent to which a memorandum of wishes is relevant to trustees. At [66], that Court says "... The settlor's wishes are always a material consideration in the exercise of fiduciary discretions. But if they were to displace all independent judgment on the part of the trustees themselves (or in the case of a corporate trustee, by its responsible officers and staff) the decision-making process would be open to serious question."

What this means is that a memorandum of wishes is relevant and should be drafted with due consideration. But also, that trustees must appraise themselves of all relevant considerations. Accordingly, when drafting a memorandum of wishes it is sensible to provide context for the wishes expressed and where relevant supporting documents so that trustees can properly consider a memorandum of wishes and if necessary, support their decision to do so.

In reviewing and amending this memorandum of wishes, it would be helpful if you could also turn your mind to your wishes in the event of your own incapacity, and to consider how the Trust would be funded and operated in these circumstances.

You should also consider your wishes for your children or whoever else you propose to benefit from the trust, including whether it is your wish that your children or such other persons are provided for from the trust fund to the extent possible, or whether it is your wish for the Trust to only provide assistance with schooling, housing, etc, or not at all until after your death. You may also like to consider whether you wish the Trustees to guide your children (if relevant) regarding making their own way in the world.

Sample Memorandum of Wishes — Single Settlor

To the Trustees of the **[Trust]**

I am the settlor of the **[Trust]** (the Trust) established by Deed dated **[date]** (the Trust Deed).

Purpose of Trust Formation

I established the Trust principally to provide general asset protection for myself and my family against future eventualities. **[If appropriate, add "and more specifically to . . .".]**

This Memorandum

This memorandum is intended for the guidance of you and any subsequent Trustee or Trustees. It is not binding upon you and is not intended in any way to fetter the discretionary powers vested in you under the Trust Deed. From time to time, I may amend my wishes in another memorandum. This memorandum and any subsequent memoranda are to be kept safe by you as these comprise core documents as that term is defined in the Trusts Act 2019.

I am aware that if beneficiaries request this, or any other memorandum of wishes, you will need to decide, by reference to the factors in s 53 of the Trusts Act, whether to provide a copy of this to any of the Trust's beneficiaries.

In this regard, I record that it is not my wish that this memorandum be widely circulated as it is personal to me as the Trust's Settlor and I have drafted this to provide guidance to the Trustees for the benefit of all of the Trust beneficiaries, over time. However, I appreciate the Trustees' legal obligations and repose our trust and confidence in you to manage and distribute my wishes in accordance with the duties you owe under the Trust Deed and the Trusts Act.

I have drafted this memorandum to encapsulate my wishes for the Trust and how it will benefit and provide for me and subsequent generations. I have written this in my own words and do not intend that what I say should be interpreted legally, but rather should be heard in my own voice written in consideration of my family, my background, my values and my reasons for how the Trust can best serve my family through subsequent generations.

Option

This replaces the memorandum of wishes dated **[date]**, or is in addition to, and should be read subject to, the memorandum of wishes dated **[date]**.

My Wishes

In making the comments that follow, I direct the Trustees to regard my interests in priority to that of any of the other beneficiaries during my lifetime.

The Trust was settled to ensure that there would be sufficient assets to provide income and capital as required for my welfare and benefit with provision for my children and remoter issue as a secondary consideration.

Children

Subject to my needs being fully provided for, I want my Trustees to provide for my children to assist with education and advancement in business. I do not want the Trust Funds to subsidise my children's lives such that they look to the Trust before looking to their own resources to advance their own wellbeing.

So far as possible, I wish the Trustees to maintain equality between my children. If a distribution is made to one child, I hope that it will be possible for a similar distribution to be made to the others, although I recognise that timing may sometimes vary depending on particular circumstances and needs.

Option

In addition, I wish my Trustees consider, where appropriate, meeting additional capital costs for each of my children for such things as the maintenance and improvement of their homes, furnishings and home appliances, suitable vehicles for their use, overseas travel and health care.

OR

I would like my Trustees to encourage my children to continue their education to tertiary level and to assist them with associated costs.

Grandchildren

Subject to the needs of my children being adequately dealt with, my Trustees should regard my grandchildren as the next priority. I also wish that my Trustees ensure that they provide assistance to my grandchildren in any careers or business activities that they may wish to undertake. I want them to be reasonably comfortable in life and I hope that the Trustees will also provide professional guidance to my grandchildren as required. In saying this, I wish to ensure the support of the Trust to assist my grandchildren in life and not to demotivate them with too much information regarding the value of the Trust's assets.

Option

I would like my Trustees to encourage my grandchildren to continue their education to tertiary level and to assist them with associated costs.

Other beneficiaries

In addition to meeting the interests of my children and grandchildren, over time, it is my wish that the Trustees provide for [ ] and in particular that the Trustees . . .

General Administration

Option

I regard it as important that the capital of the trust fund should, so far as possible, be maintained but not to the extent of developing unnecessarily large resources of capital resulting in the beneficiaries being denied adequate access to trust funds at a time and age when such funds would be of most use to them and their families.

OR

In the foreseeable future, the income should be more than sufficient to provide adequately for the needs of the various beneficiaries and the Trustees should attempt to reinvest surplus income so that the capital of the Trust is not only maintained but increases so as to maintain its real value in line with inflation.

OR

I regard the property at **[Address]** as a permanent asset of the Trust not only because I have a sentimental attachment to the property but also because I believe it will appreciate in value and keep pace with inflation. Under no circumstances should this property be sold unless the Trustees, having considered every possible alternative, reach the conclusion that they have no other choice.

Dated this day of 20

____

[Name]

11.2 Memorandum of Wishes — Joint Settlors

Notes to settlors regarding drafting a memorandum of wishes

This memorandum of wishes is in draft, for your consideration. We have prepared this memorandum based on our discussion with you. Please amend this document to reflect your wishes. Please include anything that you think is important to you about the purpose of the trust in this memorandum of wishes, even if you are unsure whether it is relevant. We can discuss any points we feel should not be included.

In considering the terms or form of your memorandum of wishes, it is important to consider why the Trust was settled, and what you intend the Trust to achieve.

Please note that this memorandum of wishes will not be binding on the Trustees, but it is highly persuasive and intended to provide guidance for the Trustees in the event you are unable to tell the Trustees what you wish them to do during your lifetime, and also after your death. Accordingly, your memorandum of wishes should be drafted following careful consideration regarding the Trust's purposes. As stated by the Court of Appeal in *Chambers v SR Hamilton Corporate Trustee Ltd* [2017] NZCA 131; (2017) 4 NZTR ¶27-008 at [36]:

> "Settlors are entitled to express their wishes for the benefit of trustees, and trustees are entitled to take them into account. They can be important guidance to them in the exercise of discretionary powers. However trustees, whatever a settlor's wishes, must conscientiously apply their independent discretion in exercising their powers. Wishes can only be taken into account if they are not inconsistent with the purposes of the trust as appear from its written terms. Trustees should not blindly obey all settlor instructions. It is necessary for trustees to read and understand a memorandum of guidance to discern the settlor's wishes, and then with those wishes in mind make an independent assessment of the appropriate course of action, taking into account not just the memoranda, but all relevant factors."

In *Pitt v Holt* [2013] 2 WLR 1200, the United Kingdom Supreme Court also reflects on the extent to which a memorandum of wishes is relevant to trustees. At [66], that Court says "... The settlor's wishes are always a material consideration in the exercise of fiduciary discretions. But if they were to displace all independent judgment on the part of the trustees themselves (or in the case of a corporate trustee, by its responsible officers and staff) the decision-making process would be open to serious question."

What this means is that a memorandum of wishes is relevant and should be drafted with due consideration. But also, that trustees must appraise themselves of all relevant considerations. Accordingly, when drafting a memorandum of wishes it is sensible to provide context for the wishes expressed and where relevant supporting documents so that trustees can properly consider a memorandum of wishes and if necessary, support their decision to do so.

In reviewing and amending this memorandum of wishes, it would be helpful if you could also turn your mind to your wishes in the event of your own incapacity, and to consider how the Trust would be funded and operated in these circumstances.

You should also consider your wishes for your children or whoever else you propose to benefit from the trust, including whether it is your wish that your children or such other persons are provided for from the trust fund to the extent possible, or whether it is your wish for the Trust to only provide assistance with schooling, housing, etc, or not at all until after your death. You may also like to consider whether you wish the Trustees to guide your children (if relevant) regarding making their own way in the world.

Separately, it is important, given how long the Trust can run, for you to consider whether, if the Trust Deed does not already provide for this, that you as Settlors, can nominate successors who can provide a memorandum of wishes after the death of the survivor of you. At the same time, if the Trust Deed does not already provide for this, it is sensible to consider whether the survivor of you can provide one or more updating memoranda of wishes.

An appropriate clause to achieve this might be:

> The Settlors, or the survivor of them, have, without in any way limiting the discretion of the Trustees, the right to provide the Trustees with a Memorandum of Wishes providing guidance to the Trustees that can be updated from time to time at the discretion of the Settlors, or the survivor of them.

Sample Memorandum of Wishes — Joint Settlors

To the Trustees of the **[Trust]**

We are the Settlors of the **[Trust]** (the Trust) established by Deed dated **[date]** (the Trust Deed).

Purpose of Trust Formation

We established the Trust principally to provide general asset protection for ourselves and our family against future eventualities. **[If appropriate, add "and more specifically to . . .".]**

This Memorandum

This memorandum is intended for the guidance of you and any subsequent Trustee or Trustees. It is not binding upon you and is not intended in any way to fetter the discretionary powers vested in you under the Trust Deed. From time to time, we may amend our wishes in another memorandum. This memorandum and any subsequent memoranda are to be kept safe by you as these comprise core documents as that term is defined in the Trusts Act 2019.

We are also aware that if beneficiaries request this, or any other memorandum of wishes, you will need to decide, by reference to the factors in s 53 of the Trusts Act, whether to provide a copy of this to any of the Trust's beneficiaries.

In this regard, we record that it is not our wish that this memorandum be widely circulated as it is personal to us as Settlors and we have drafted this to provide guidance to the Trustees for the benefit of all of the Trust beneficiaries, over time. However, we appreciate the Trustees' legal obligations and repose our trust and confidence in you to manage and distribute our wishes in accordance with the duties you owe under the Trust Deed Trust and the Trusts Act.

We have drafted this memorandum to encapsulate our wishes for the Trust and how it will benefit and provide for us and subsequent generations. We have written this in our own words and do not intend that what we say should be interpreted legally, but rather should be heard in our voice written in consideration of our family, our background, our values and our reasons for how the Trust can best serve our family through subsequent generations.

Option

This replaces the memorandum of wishes dated **[date]**, or is in addition to, and should be read subject to, the memorandum of wishes dated **[date]**.

Our Wishes

In making the comments that follow, we direct the Trustees to regard the interests of each of the Settlors in priority to that of any of the other beneficiaries during our lifetime.

The Trust was settled to ensure that there would be sufficient assets to provide income and capital as required for our welfare and benefit with provision for our children and remoter issue as a secondary consideration.

Children

Subject to our needs being fully provided for, we want our Trustees to provide for our children to assist with education and advancement in business. We do not want the Trust Funds to subsidise our children's lives such that they look to the Trust before looking to their own resources to advance their own wellbeing.

So far as possible, we wish the Trustees to maintain equality between our children. If a distribution is made to one child, we hope that it will be possible for a similar distribution to be made to the others, although we recognise that timing may sometimes vary depending on particular circumstances and needs.

Option

In addition, we wish our Trustees to consider, if appropriate, meeting additional capital costs for each of our children for such things as the maintenance and improvement of their homes, furnishings and home appliances, suitable vehicles for their use, overseas travel and health care.

OR

We would like our Trustees to encourage our children to continue their education to tertiary level and to assist them with associated costs.

Grandchildren

Subject to the needs of our children being adequately dealt with, our Trustees should regard our grandchildren as the next priority. We also wish our Trustees to ensure that they provide assistance to our grandchildren in any careers or business activities that they may wish to undertake. We want them to be reasonably comfortable in life and we hope that the Trustees will also provide professional guidance to our grandchildren as required. In saying this, we wish to ensure the support of the Trust to assist our grandchildren in life and not to demotivate them with too much information regarding the value of the Trust's assets.

Option

We would like our Trustees to encourage our grandchildren to continue their education to tertiary level and to assist them with associated costs.

Other beneficiaries

In addition to meeting the interests of our children and grandchildren, over time, it is our wish that the Trustees provide for [ ] and in particular that the Trustees . . .

General Administration

Option

We regard it as important that the capital of the trust fund should, so far as possible, be maintained but not to the extent of developing unnecessarily large resources of capital resulting in the beneficiaries being denied adequate access to trust funds at a time and age when such funds would be of most use to them and their families.

OR

In the foreseeable future, the income should be more than sufficient to provide adequately for the needs of the various beneficiaries and the Trustees should attempt to reinvest surplus income so that the capital of the Trust is not only maintained but increases so as to maintain its real value in line with inflation.

OR

We regard the property at **[Address]** as a permanent asset of the Trust not only because we have a sentimental attachment to the property but also because we believe it will appreciate in value and keep pace with inflation. Under no circumstances should this property be sold unless the Trustees, having considered every possible alternative, reach the conclusion that they have no other choice.

Dated this day of 20

____

[Name]

____

[Name]

11.3 Memorandum of Wishes — Economic Settlor

Notes to settlor regarding drafting a memorandum of wishes

This memorandum of wishes is in draft, for your consideration. We have prepared this memorandum based on our discussion with you. Please amend this document to reflect your wishes. Please include anything that you think is important to you about the purpose of the trust in this memorandum of wishes, even if you are unsure whether it is relevant. We can discuss any points we feel should not be included.

In considering the terms or form of your memorandum of wishes, it is important to consider why the Trust was settled, and what you intend the Trust to achieve.

You should also consider your wishes for yourself as an economic settlor of the trust and the source of the trust wealth, as well as for the other beneficiaries of the trust. It may be relevant to also set out why you are not named as a settlor and the circumstances in which the trust was settled.

Please note that this memorandum of wishes will not be binding on the Trustees, but it is highly persuasive and intended to provide guidance for the Trustees in the event you are unable to tell the Trustees what you wish them to do during your lifetime, and also after your death. Accordingly, your memorandum of wishes should be drafted following careful consideration regarding the Trust's purposes. As stated by the Court of Appeal in *Chambers v SR Hamilton Corporate Trustee Ltd* [2017] NZCA 131; (2017) 4 NZTR ¶27-008 at [36]:

> "Settlors are entitled to express their wishes for the benefit of trustees, and trustees are entitled to take them into account. They can be important guidance to them in the exercise of discretionary powers. However trustees, whatever a settlor's wishes, must conscientiously apply their independent discretion in exercising their powers. Wishes can only be taken into account if they are not inconsistent with the purposes of the trust as appear from its written terms. Trustees should not blindly obey all settlor instructions. It is necessary for trustees to read and understand a memorandum of guidance to discern the settlor's wishes, and then with those wishes in mind make an independent assessment of the appropriate course of action, taking into account not just the memoranda, but all relevant factors."

In *Pitt v Holt* [2013] 2 WLR 1200, the United Kingdom Supreme Court also reflects on the extent to which a memorandum of wishes is relevant to trustees. At [66], that Court says "... The settlor's wishes are always a material consideration in the exercise of fiduciary discretions. But if they were to displace all independent judgment on the part of the trustees themselves (or in the case of a corporate trustee, by its responsible officers and staff) the decision-making process would be open to serious question."

What this means is that a memorandum of wishes is relevant and should be drafted with due consideration. But also, that trustees must appraise themselves of all relevant considerations. Accordingly, when drafting a memorandum of wishes it is sensible to provide context for the wishes expressed and where relevant supporting documents so that trustees can properly consider a memorandum of wishes and if necessary, support their decision to do so.

In reviewing and amending this memorandum of wishes, it would be helpful if you could also turn your mind to your wishes in the event of your own incapacity, and to consider how the Trust would be funded and operated in these circumstances.

You should also consider your wishes for your children or whoever else you propose to benefit from the trust, including whether it is your wish that your children or such other persons are provided for from the trust fund to the extent possible, or whether it is your wish for the Trust to only provide assistance with schooling, housing, etc, or not at all until after your death. You may also like to consider whether you wish the Trustees to guide your children (if relevant) regarding making their own way in the world.

Sample Memorandum of Wishes — Economic Settlor

To the Trustees of the **[Trust]**

I am the economic settlor of the **[Trust]** (the Trust) established by Deed dated **[date]** (the Trust Deed).

Purpose of Trust Formation

I arranged for the Trust to be established because it was my wish that there would be a trust that would provide general asset protection for settlements that I would make onto the trust for the benefit of the named beneficiaries.

This Memorandum

This memorandum is intended for the guidance of you and any subsequent Trustee or Trustees. It is not binding upon you and is not intended in any way to fetter the discretionary powers vested in you under the Trust Deed. From time to time, I may amend my wishes in another memorandum. This memorandum and any subsequent memoranda are to be kept safe by you as these comprise core documents as that term is defined in the Trusts Act 2019.

I am aware that if beneficiaries request this, or any other memorandum of wishes, you will need to decide, by reference to the factors in s 53 of the Trusts Act, whether to provide a copy of this to any of the Trust's beneficiaries.

In this regard, I record that it is not my wish that this memorandum be widely circulated as it is personal to me as the economic settlor and I have drafted this to provide guidance to the Trustees for the benefit of all of the Trust's beneficiaries, over time.

I appreciate the Trustees' legal obligations and repose our trust and confidence in you to manage and distribute my wishes in accordance with the duties you owe under the Trust Deed Trust and the Trusts Act.

I have drafted this memorandum to encapsulate my wishes for the Trust and how I wish that it will benefit and provide for me and the other named beneficiaries. I have written this in my own words and do not intend that what I say should be interpreted legally, but rather should be heard in our voice written in consideration of my family, my background, my values and my reasons for how the Trust can best serve the beneficiaries through subsequent generations.

Option

This replaces the memorandum of wishes dated **[date]**, or is in addition to, and should be read subject to, the memorandum of wishes dated **[date]**.

11.3

My Wishes

The Trust was settled to ensure that there would be sufficient assets to provide income and capital as required for the welfare and benefit of myself as the economic settlor of the trust with provision for the other named beneficiaries as a secondary consideration.

Children

Subject to my needs being fully provided for, it is my wish that the Trustees provide for my children to assist with education and advancement in business. I do not want the Trust Funds to subsidise my children's lives such that they look to the Trust before looking to their own resources to advance their own wellbeing.

So far as possible, it is my wish that the Trustees maintain equality between my children. If a distribution is made to one child, I hope that it will be possible for a similar distribution to be made to the others, although I recognise that timing may sometimes vary depending on particular circumstances and needs.

Option

In addition, I wish that my Trustees consider, where appropriate, meeting additional capital costs for each of my children for such things as the maintenance and improvement of their homes, furnishings and home appliances, suitable vehicles for their use, overseas travel and health care.

OR

I would like the Trustees to encourage my children to continue their education to tertiary level and to assist them with associated costs.

Grandchildren

Subject to the needs of my children being adequately dealt with, the Trustees should regard my grandchildren as the next priority. I also wish that the Trustees ensure that they provide assistance to my grandchildren in any careers or business activities that they may wish to undertake. I want them to be reasonably comfortable in life and I hope that the Trustees will also provide professional guidance to my grandchildren as required. In saying this, I wish to ensure the support of the Trust to assist my grandchildren in life and not to demotivate them with too much information regarding the value of the Trust's assets.

Option

I would like the Trustees to encourage my grandchildren to continue their education to tertiary level and to assist them with associated costs.

Other beneficiaries

In addition to meeting the interests of my children and grandchildren, over time, it is my wish that the Trustees provide for [ ] and in particular that the Trustees . . .

General Administration

Option

I regard it as important that the capital of the trust fund should, so far as possible, be maintained but not to the extent of developing unnecessarily large resources of capital resulting in the beneficiaries being denied adequate access to trust funds at a time and age when such funds would be of most use to them and their families.

OR

In the foreseeable future, the income should be more than sufficient to provide adequately for the needs of the various beneficiaries and the Trustees should attempt to reinvest surplus income so that the capital of the Trust is not only maintained but increases so as to maintain its real value in line with inflation.

OR

I regard the property at **[Address]** as a permanent asset of the Trust. Under no circumstances should this property be sold unless the Trustees, having considered every possible alternative, reach the conclusion that they have no other choice.

Dated this day of 20

____

[Name]

11.4 Memorandum of Wishes — Economic Settlors

Notes to settlor regarding drafting a memorandum of wishes

This memorandum of wishes is in draft, for your consideration. We have prepared this memorandum based on our discussion with you. Please amend this document to reflect your wishes. Please include anything that you think is important to you about the purpose of the trust in this memorandum of wishes, even if you are unsure whether it is relevant. We can discuss any points we feel should not be included.

In considering the terms or form of your memorandum of wishes, it is important to consider why the Trust was settled, and what you intend the Trust to achieve.

You should also consider your wishes for yourselves as the economic settlors of the trust and the source of the trust wealth, as well as for the other beneficiaries of the trust. It may be relevant to also set out why you are not named as a settlors and the circumstances in which the trust was settled.

Please note that this memorandum of wishes will not be binding on the Trustees, but it is highly persuasive and intended to provide guidance for the Trustees in the event you are unable to tell the Trustees what you wish them to do during your lifetime, and also after your death. Accordingly, your memorandum of wishes should be drafted following careful consideration regarding the Trust's purposes. As stated by the Court of Appeal in *Chambers v SR Hamilton Corporate Trustee Ltd* [2017] NZCA 131; (2017) 4 NZTR ¶27-008 at [36]:

> "Settlors are entitled to express their wishes for the benefit of trustees, and trustees are entitled to take them into account. They can be important guidance to them in the exercise of discretionary powers. However trustees, whatever a settlor's wishes, must conscientiously apply their independent discretion in exercising their powers. Wishes can only be taken into account if they are not inconsistent with the purposes of the trust as appear from its written terms. Trustees should not blindly obey all settlor instructions. It is necessary for trustees to read and understand a memorandum of guidance to discern the settlor's wishes, and then with those wishes in mind make an independent assessment of the appropriate course of action, taking into account not just the memoranda, but all relevant factors."

In *Pitt v Holt* [2013] 2 WLR 1200, the United Kingdom Supreme Court also reflects on the extent to which a memorandum of wishes is relevant to trustees. At [66], that Court says ". . . The settlor's wishes are always a material consideration in the exercise of fiduciary discretions. But if they were to displace all independent judgment on the part of the trustees themselves (or in the case of a corporate trustee, by its responsible officers and staff) the decision-making process would be open to serious question."

What this means is that a memorandum of wishes is relevant and should be drafted with due consideration. But also, that trustees must appraise themselves of all relevant considerations. Accordingly, when drafting a memorandum of wishes it is sensible to provide context for the wishes expressed and where relevant supporting documents so that trustees can properly consider a memorandum of wishes and if necessary, support their decision to do so.

In reviewing and amending this memorandum of wishes, it would be helpful if you could also turn your mind to your wishes in the event of your own incapacity, and to consider how the Trust would be funded and operated in these circumstances.

You should also consider your wishes for your children or whoever else you propose to benefit from the trust, including whether it is your wish that your children or such other persons are provided for from the trust fund to the extent possible, or whether it is your wish for the Trust to only provide assistance with schooling, housing, etc, or not at all until after your death. You may also like to consider whether you wish the Trustees to guide your children (if relevant) regarding making their own way in the world.

Sample Memorandum of Wishes — Economic Settlors

To the Trustees of the **[Trust]**

We are the economic settlors of the **[Trust]** (the Trust) established by Deed dated **[date]** (the Trust Deed).

Purpose of Trust Formation

We arranged for the Trust to be established because it was our wish that there would be a trust that would provide general asset protection for settlements that we would make onto the trust for the benefit of the named beneficiaries.

This Memorandum

This memorandum is intended for the guidance of you and any subsequent Trustee or Trustees. It is not binding upon you and is not intended in any way to fetter the discretionary powers vested in you under the Trust Deed. From time to time, we may amend our wishes in another memorandum. This memorandum and any subsequent memoranda are to be kept safe by you as these comprise core documents as that term is defined in the Trusts Act 2019.

We are aware that if beneficiaries request this, or any other memorandum of wishes, you will need to decide, by reference to the factors in s 53 of the Trusts Act, whether to provide a copy of this to any of the Trust's beneficiaries.

In this regard, we record that it is not our wish that this memorandum be widely circulated as it is personal to us as the economic settlors and we have drafted this to provide guidance to the Trustees for the benefit of all of the Trust's beneficiaries, over time.

We appreciate the Trustees' legal obligations and repose our trust and confidence in you to manage and distribute our wishes in accordance with the duties you owe under the Trust Deed Trust and the Trusts Act.

We have drafted this memorandum to encapsulate our wishes for the Trust and how we wish that it will benefit and provide for us and the other named beneficiaries. We have written this in our own words and do not intend that what we say should be interpreted legally, but rather should be heard in our voices written in consideration of our family, our backgrounds, our values and our reasons for how the Trust can best serve the beneficiaries through subsequent generations.

Option

This replaces the memorandum of wishes dated **[date]**, or is in addition to, and should be read subject to, the memorandum of wishes dated **[date]**.

Our Wishes

The Trust was settled to ensure that there would be sufficient assets to provide income and capital as required for the welfare and benefit of ourselves as the economic settlors of the trust with provision for the other named beneficiaries as a secondary consideration.

Children

Subject to our needs (or the needs of the survivor of us) being fully provided for, it is our wish that the Trustees provide for our children to assist with education and advancement in business.

We do not want the Trust Funds to subsidise our children's lives such that they look to the Trust before looking to their own resources to advance their own wellbeing.

So far as possible, it is our wish that the Trustees maintain equality between our children. If a distribution is made to one child, we hope that it will be possible for a similar distribution to be made to the others, although we recognise that timing may sometimes vary depending on particular circumstances and needs.

Option

In addition, we wish our Trustees to consider, if appropriate, meeting additional capital costs for each of our children for such things as the maintenance and improvement of their homes, furnishings and home appliances, suitable vehicles for their use, overseas travel and health care.

OR

We would like the Trustees to encourage our children to continue their education to tertiary level and to assist them with associated costs.

Grandchildren

Subject to the needs of our children being adequately dealt with, the Trustees should regard our grandchildren as the next priority. We also wish that the Trustees ensure that they provide assistance to our grandchildren in any careers or business activities that they may wish to undertake. We want them to be reasonably comfortable in life and we hope that the Trustees will also provide professional guidance to our grandchildren as required. In saying this, we wish to ensure the support of the Trust to assist our grandchildren in life and not to demotivate them with too much information regarding the value of the Trust's assets.

Option

We would like the Trustees to encourage our grandchildren to continue their education to tertiary level and to assist them with associated costs.

Other beneficiaries

In addition to meeting the interests of our children and grandchildren, over time, it is our wish that the Trustees provide for [ ] and in particular that the Trustees . . .

General Administration

Option

We regard it as important that the capital of the trust fund should, so far as possible, be maintained but not to the extent of developing unnecessarily large resources of capital resulting in the beneficiaries being denied adequate access to trust funds at a time and age when such funds would be of most use to them and their families.

OR

In the foreseeable future, the income should be more than sufficient to provide adequately for the needs of the various beneficiaries and the Trustees should attempt to reinvest surplus income so that the capital of the Trust is not only maintained but increases so as to maintain its real value in line with inflation.

OR

We regard the property at **[Address]** as a permanent asset of the Trust. Under no circumstances should this property be sold unless the Trustees, having considered every possible alternative, reach the conclusion that they have no other choice.

Dated this day of 20

____

[Name]

____

[Name]

11.5 Simple Memorandum of Wishes — Single Settlor

Notes to the settlor regarding drafting a memorandum of wishes

This memorandum of wishes is provided in "tick box" format to assist you to set out your wishes as settlor.

This memorandum of wishes is in draft, for your consideration. We have prepared this memorandum based on our discussion with you. Please amend this document to reflect your wishes. Please include anything that you think is important to you about the purpose of the trust in this memorandum of wishes, even if you are unsure whether it is relevant. We can discuss any points we feel should not be included.

In considering the terms or form of your memorandum of wishes, it is important to consider why the Trust was settled, and what you intend the Trust to achieve.

Please note that this memorandum of wishes will not be binding on the Trustees, but it is highly persuasive and intended to provide guidance for the Trustees in the event you are unable to tell the Trustees what you wish them to do during your lifetime, and also after your death. Accordingly, your memorandum of wishes should be drafted following careful consideration regarding the Trust's purposes. As stated by the Court of Appeal in *Chambers v SR Hamilton Corporate Trustee Ltd* [2017] NZCA 131; (2017) 4 NZTR ¶27-008 at [36]:

> "Settlors are entitled to express their wishes for the benefit of trustees, and trustees are entitled to take them into account. They can be important guidance to them in the exercise of discretionary powers. However trustees, whatever a settlor's wishes, must conscientiously apply their independent discretion in exercising their powers. Wishes can only be taken into account if they are not inconsistent with the purposes of the trust as appear from its written terms. Trustees should not blindly obey all settlor instructions. It is necessary for trustees to read and understand a memorandum of guidance to discern the settlor's wishes, and then with those wishes in mind make an independent assessment of the appropriate course of action, taking into account not just the memoranda, but all relevant factors."

In *Pitt v Holt* [2013] 2 WLR 1200, the United Kingdom Supreme Court also reflects on the extent to which a memorandum of wishes is relevant to trustees. At [66], that Court says "... The settlor's wishes are always a material consideration in the exercise of fiduciary discretions. But if they were to displace all independent judgment on the part of the trustees themselves (or in the case of a corporate trustee, by its responsible officers and staff) the decision-making process would be open to serious question."

What this means is that a memorandum of wishes is relevant and should be drafted with due consideration. But also, that trustees must appraise themselves of all relevant considerations. Accordingly, when drafting a memorandum of wishes it is sensible to provide context for the wishes expressed and where relevant supporting documents so that trustees can properly consider a memorandum of wishes and if necessary, support their decision to do so.

In reviewing and amending this memorandum of wishes, it would be helpful if you could also turn your mind to your wishes in the event of your own incapacity, and to consider how the Trust would be funded and operated in these circumstances.

You should also consider your wishes for your children or whoever else you propose to benefit from the trust, including whether it is your wish that your children or such other persons are provided for from the trust fund to the extent possible, or whether it is your wish for the Trust to only provide assistance with schooling, housing, etc, or not at all until after your death. You may also like to consider whether you wish the Trustees to guide your children (if relevant) regarding making their own way in the world.

While this draft memorandum of wishes is simple in format, it can be amended as required by you to fully reflect your wishes and can be updated by you when appropriate to do so.

Sample Memorandum of Wishes — Single Settlor — Simple Option

To: the trustees of the Trust (the Trust)

Dear Trustees

I do not wish to fetter your discretionary powers as trustees. However, I would like you to take my wishes, as set out below, into consideration for the future administration of the Trust. It is my intention to review the terms of this Memorandum of Wishes on a regular basis. That said, unless or until I do, the wishes expressed herein are my wishes.

During my lifetime, I should like you to be guided by these wishes (unless or until they are updated) with regard to the distribution of income or capital of the trust.

I acknowledge the presumption that trustees will make basic trust information (as that term is defined in the Trusts Act 2019) available to all beneficiaries but do not want the following beneficiaries to be given basic trust information or disclosure of trust information because: [expand]

I attach a family tree.

☐ During my lifetime, I direct you to prefer my interests ahead of any other beneficiaries of the Trust.

☐ During my lifetime, I direct you to consider my interests together with the other beneficiaries of the Trust with no expectation by me that my interests will be prioritised because I have settled assets onto the Trust.

Following my death, it is my wish that the beneficiaries referred to below benefit from the Trust to the extent specified.

Name:

Address:

Relationship to the settlor:

Date of birth

____ % of the Trust Fund

Age to benefit ____

Name:

Address:

Relationship to the settlor:

Date of birth

____ % of the Trust Fund

Age to benefit ____

Each beneficiary referred to above must attain the "Age to benefit" before receiving any distribution of Trust assets. However, please consider using the Trust assets to provide for the welfare of any beneficiary before the Age to benefit. In these circumstances, please consult with:

Name:

Relationship:

Address:

If any beneficiary dies without issue, the share that should have gone to that beneficiary should be distributed:

[____] evenly amongst the surviving beneficiaries referred to above

[____] to [name]

Signed:

Date:

Family tree

template.net/editable/66635/3-generation-family-genogram

11.6 Simple Memorandum of Wishes — Two Settlors

Notes to the settlors regarding drafting a memorandum of wishes

This memorandum of wishes is provided in "tick box" format to assist you to set out your wishes as settlor.

This memorandum of wishes is in draft, for your consideration. We have prepared this memorandum based on our discussion with you. Please amend this document to reflect your wishes. Please include anything that you think is important to you about the purpose of the trust in this memorandum of wishes, even if you are unsure whether it is relevant. We can discuss any points we feel should not be included.

In considering the terms or form of your memorandum of wishes, it is important to consider why the Trust was settled, and what you intend the Trust to achieve.

Please note that this memorandum of wishes will not be binding on the Trustees, but it is highly persuasive and intended to provide guidance for the Trustees in the event you are unable to tell the Trustees what you wish them to do during your lifetime, and also after your death. Accordingly, your memorandum of wishes should be drafted following careful consideration regarding the Trust's purposes. As stated by the Court of Appeal in *Chambers v SR Hamilton Corporate Trustee Ltd* [2017] NZCA 131; (2017) 4 NZTR ¶27-008 at [36]:

> "Settlors are entitled to express their wishes for the benefit of trustees, and trustees are entitled to take them into account. They can be important guidance to them in the exercise of discretionary powers. However trustees, whatever a settlor's wishes, must conscientiously apply their independent discretion in exercising their powers. Wishes can only be taken into account if they are not inconsistent with the purposes of the trust as appear from its written terms. Trustees should not blindly obey all settlor instructions. It is necessary for trustees to read and understand a memorandum of guidance to discern the settlor's wishes, and then with those wishes in mind make an independent assessment of the appropriate course of action, taking into account not just the memoranda, but all relevant factors."

In *Pitt v Holt* [2013] 2 WLR 1200, the United Kingdom Supreme Court also reflects on the extent to which a memorandum of wishes is relevant to trustees. At [66], that Court says "... The settlor's wishes are always a material consideration in the exercise of fiduciary discretions. But if they were to displace all independent judgment on the part of the trustees themselves (or in the case of a corporate trustee, by its responsible officers and staff) the decision-making process would be open to serious question."

What this means is that a memorandum of wishes is relevant and should be drafted with due consideration. But also, that trustees must appraise themselves of all relevant considerations. Accordingly, when drafting a memorandum of wishes it is sensible to provide context for the wishes expressed and where relevant supporting documents so that trustees can properly consider a memorandum of wishes and if necessary, support their decision to do so.

In reviewing and amending this memorandum of wishes, it would be helpful if you could also turn your mind to your wishes in the event of your own incapacity, and to consider how the Trust would be funded and operated in these circumstances.

You should also consider your wishes for your children or whoever else you propose to benefit from the trust, including whether it is your wish that your children or such other persons are provided for from the trust fund to the extent possible, or whether it is your wish for the Trust to only provide assistance with schooling, housing, etc, or not at all until after your death. You may also like to consider whether you wish the Trustees to guide your children (if relevant) regarding making their own way in the world.

While this draft memorandum of wishes is simple in format, it can be amended as required by you to fully reflect your wishes and can be updated by you when appropriate to do so.

Sample Memorandum of Wishes — Two Settlors — Simple Option

To: the trustees of the Trust (the Trust)

Dear Trustees

We do not wish to fetter your discretionary powers as trustees. However, we would like you to take our wishes, as set out below, into consideration for the future administration of the Trust. It is our intention to review the terms of this Memorandum of Wishes on a regular basis. However, unless or until we do, the wishes expressed herein are my wishes.

During the lifetime of both of us and then the survivor of us we should like you to be guided by these wishes (unless or until they are updated) with regard to the distribution of income or capital of the trust.

We acknowledge presumption that trustees will make basic trust information available to all beneficiaries but do not want the following beneficiaries to be given basic trust information or disclosure of trust information because: [expand]

We attach a family tree.

☐ During our lifetime we direct you to prefer our interests ahead of any other beneficiaries of the Trust.

☐ In the event of the death of one of us, we should like the Trust assets to be fully available to the survivor of us.

☐ In the event of the death of one of us, it is our wish that you prefer the interests of the survivor of us ahead of any other beneficiaries of the Trust.

Following the death of both of us, it is our wish that the beneficiaries referred to below benefit from the Trust to the extent specified.

Name:

Address:

Relationship to the settlors

Date of birth

____ % of the Trust Fund

Age to benefit ____

Each beneficiary referred to above must attain the age to benefit before receiving any distribution of Trust assets. However, please consider using the Trust assets to provide for the welfare of any beneficiary before the age to benefit. In these circumstances, please consult with:

Name:

Relationship:

Address:

If any beneficiary shall die without issue, the share that should have gone to that child should be distributed evenly amongst the surviving beneficiaries referred to above.

Signed:

Date:

Signed:

Date:

Family tree

template.net/editable/66635/3-generation-family-genogram

Case Table

Paragraph

A

Abacus Trust Co (Isle of Man) v Barr [2003] EWHC 114; [2003] Ch 409; [2003] 1 All ER 763 ... 5.2; 5.5; 10.3
Addleman v Lambie Trustee Ltd [2017] NZHC 2054; (2017) 4 NZTR ¶27-016 ... 7.1

B

Bank of Nova Scotia v Borletta (1994) 1 JIP 35 ... 3.6; 3.11
Banks v Goodfellow (1870) LR 5 QB 549 ... 9.3
Beloved Wilke's Charity, Re [1851] EWHC Ch J52 42 ER 330 ... 6.7
Breakspear v Ackland [2008] EWHC 220 (Ch); [2009] Ch 32 ... 1.4; 2.1; 2.3; 4.1; 5.1; 5.3

C

C Trust, Re the [2012] JRC 086B ... 3.5; 3.10; 5.1; 5.3
Carson v Lane [2019] NZHC 3259; (2019) 5 NZTR ¶29-038 ... 5.2
Chambers v SR Hamilton Corporate Trustee Ltd [2017] NZCA 131; (2017) 4 NZTR ¶27-008 ... 3.3; 3.11; 3.12; 3.14; 5.3; 11.1–11.5
Chapman, Re (1985) 72 LT 67 ... 3.16
Chirnside v Fay [2006] NZSC 68; (2006) 8 NZBLC 101,831 ... 9.2
Clayton v Clayton [2015] NZCA 30; (2015) 4 NZTR ¶25-001 ... 9.2
Clayton v Clayton [Vaughan Road Property Trust] [2016] NZSC 29; (2016) 4 NZTR ¶26-002 ... 1.8
Clement v Lucas [2017] NZHC 3278; (2017) 4 NZTR ¶27-035 ... 8.1; 10.3
Collins Family Trust, Re; Walker & Ors v Collins & Anor [2009] NZHC 225; (2009) 2 NZTR ¶19-004 ... 5.1; 5.3
Cowin, Re (1886) 33 Ch D 179 (Ch) ... 6.7

D

Dever v Knobloch [2009] NZHC 2013; (2009) 2 NZTR ¶19-042 ... 3.6

E

E, L, O & R Trusts, Re [2010] WTLR 31 ... 5.1; 5.3
Erceg v Erceg [2015] NZHC 594; (2015) 4 NZTR ¶25-010 ... 4.3.2
Erceg v Erceg [2016] NZCA 7; [2016] NZSC 69; (2016) 4 NZTR ¶26-001 ... 4.3.1; 4.3.2
Erceg v Erceg [2017] NZSC 28; (2017) 4 NZTR ¶27-003 ... 4.2; 4.3.1 ; 4.3.3 ; 4.4 ; 4.6; 6.7
Esteem Settlement, Re [2003] JLR 188 ... 3.14; 5.5

F

Foreman v Kingstone (2003) 1 NZTR ¶13-018; [2004] 1 NZLR 841 ... 4.3.3; 6.7

G

GB Trustees Ltd v Stock [2021] JRC 048 ... 3.14
Gailey v Gordon (2003) 1 NZTR ¶13-002 ... 8.1
Gestetner Settlement, In re [1953] Ch 672 ... 2.2
Green v Green [2016] NZCA 486; (2016) 4 NZTR ¶26-021 ... 9.1; 9.4

H

Harrison v Harrison [2015] NZHC 2935; (2015) 4 NZTR ¶25-029 ... 1.6; 3.3; 5.3
Harrison v Rowan 3 Washington, 585 ... 9.3

Paragraph

Hartigan Nominees Pty Ltd v Rydge (1992) 29 NSWLR 405 .... 3.3; 4.6; 6.7; 7.3
Hay's Settlement Trusts, Re [1981] 3 All ER 786 (Ch D) 3.7; 3.13

I

Investec Co-Trustees (Jersey) Ltd v Kidd [2012] JRC 066 .... 3.14

J

Jacomb v Jacomb [2020] NZHC 1764; (2020) 5 NZTR ¶30-010 .... 4.7; 6.7
Jay v Jay [2014] NZCA 445; [2015] NZAR 861 .... 9.2

K

Kain v Hutton (No 2) (2004) 1 NZTR ¶14-022 .... 3.2; 3.3; 3.12
Kain v Hutton [2007] NZCA 199; (2007) 2 NZTR ¶17-009 .... 3.3; 3.4; 3.9; 3.13
Kain v Public Trust [2021] NZCA 685; (2021) 5 NZTR ¶31-020 .... 2.1; 5.4; 5.5
King, The v The Archbishop of Canterbury (15 East, 117) 6.7

L

Londonderry's Settlement, Re [1964] EWCA Civ 6 .... 6.7

M

McGuire v Earl [2020] NZHC 3083; (2020) 5 NZTR ¶30-025 .... 4.8
McGuire v Earl [2021] NZHC 129 (costs judgment). 4.8
Mackie Law Independent Trustee Ltd v Chaplow [2017] NZHC 1570; (2017) 4 NZTR ¶27-025 .... 3.15; 3.16
McLaren v McLaren [2017] NZHC 161; (2017) 4 NZTR ¶27-004 .... 9.2
McPhail v Doulton [1971] AC 424 (HL) 5.5
Manisty's Settlement, Re [1973] 2 All ER 1203 (Ch D) 3.7; 3.13; 8.1
Manisty's Settlement, Re [1974] Ch 17 .... 2.2
Marley & Ors v Mutual Security Merchant Bank and Trust Co Ltd [1991] All ER 198 (PC) 3.11
Masters v Stewart (2014) 3 NZTR ¶24-017 .... 10.3

O

O'Rourke v Darbishire [1920] AC 581 (HL) 4.6

P

Penson v Forbes [2014] NZHC 2160; (2014) 3 NZTR ¶24-026 .... 8.1
Piedmont Trust and the Riviera Trust, Re the [2021] JRC 248 .... 3.13; 3.14; 3.15
Pitt v Holt [2013] UKSC 26; [2013] 2 WLR 1200; [2013] 2 AC 108 ..... 1.6; 3.3; 3.14; 5.3; 10.3; 11.1–11.5
Public Trust v Kain [2021] NZHC 1000; (2021) 5 NZTR ¶31-002 .... 3.3; 5.3; 5.4; 9.5; 10.1

R

Rabaiotti 1989 Settlement, Re [2000] JLR 173; [2000] WTLR 953 .... 3.14
Rabaiotti Settlement, Re [2000] JRC 90 .... 4.2
Representation of Rysaffe Fiduciaires Sarl, Re the [2021] JRC 230 .... 3.14

S

SR Hamilton Corporate Trustee Ltd v White [2016] NZHC 1408; (2016) 4 NZTR ¶26-013 .... 9.1
Schmidt v Rosewood Trust Ltd [2003] UKPC 26 .... 2.2; 4.3.3; 5.5; 6.7
Spencer v Spencer [2013] NZCA 449; (2013) 3 NZTR ¶23-014 .... 3.16

Paragraph

T

Tarasiewicz v Titford [2013] NZHC 3466; (2013) 3 NZTR ¶23-020 .... 1.2
Turner v Turner [1984] 1 Ch 100 .... 8.1

V

Vestey's Executor v IRC (1949) 31 TC 1 .... 2.2

W

Walker & Ors v Collins & Anor; Collins Family Trust, Re [2009] NZHC 225; (2009) 2 NZTR ¶19-004 .... 5.1; 5.3
Webb v Webb [2020] UKPC 22; (2020) 5 NZTR ¶30-011 .... 1.2

Index

Paragraph

B

Beneficiaries
balancing interests ... 3.13
direction proceedings ... 3.14
disclosure ... 4.4
legal considerations ... 3.14
memoranda of wishes, disclosing ... 4.1
trustees owe fiduciary obligations ... 3.13
trust information ... 6.2

C

Capacity considerations, memoranda of wishes ... 9.1
clear ownership of wishes ... 9.5
context of ... 9.3
practical ... 9.6
trust context ... 9.4

Core documents
letter or memorandum of wishes ... 6.1
memoranda of wishes ... 6.8
privacy considerations ... 6.7
trust information ... 6.2; 6.4

Costs
memorandum of wishes ... 3.16

Court
disclosure of memorandum of wishes ... 4.2
trustees' decision ... 10.3
trustee's exercise of discretion ... 3.13

D

Decisions
High Court and Court of Appeal ... 4.3.2
Supreme Court ... 4.3.3
trustees ... 3.9; 6.3

Disclosure
context of request ... 4.6
Erceg v Erceg
– background ... 4.3.1
– High Court and Court of Appeal decisions ... 4.3.2
– Supreme Court decision ... 4.3.3
interests of beneficiaries ... 4.4
memoranda of wishes to beneficiaries ... 4.1
trustees ... 4.8
trust information ... 4.4
Trusts Act 2019 ... 4.2

Discretionary trusts ... 2.2

Paragraph

Documents
memorandum of wishes ... 2.3
rudimentary ... 4.7

Drafting memorandum of wishes
economic settlor ... 11.3
essential narrative ... 10.3
joint settlors ... 11.2
matters to take into consideration ... 10.4
multiple trusts ... 10.2
settlor/settlors ... 10.1
settlors' wishes ... 10.3
single settlor ... 11.1

E

Economic settlors ... 7.1–7.4
beneficiaries ... 11.3
drafting memorandum of wishes ... 11.3
general administration ... 11.3
trust formation ... 11.3

F

Fiduciary considerations
memorandum of wishes ... 9.2

Fiduciary obligations
imputation ... 9.2
trustees ... 3.7

J

Joint settlors
beneficiaries ... 11.2
drafting memorandum of wishes ... 11.2
general administration ... 11.2
simple option ... 11.6
trust formation ... 11.2

L

Language
judicial support for memoranda of wishes ... 3.3

M

Memorandum of wishes
as core documents ... 6.1; 6.8
– not necessarily trust information ... 6.4
– procedure for deciding whether presumption applies ... 6.6

Paragraph

Memorandum of wishes—continued
– Trust Act ... 6.7
– trustees, trust information on request.... 6.2; 6.5
– trust information, not include reasons for trustees' decisions ... 6.3
capacity ... 9.1; 9.3; 9.4
– practical considerations ... 9.6
categorisation ... 4.5
clear ownership of wishes ... 9.5
consideration for trustees ... 1.7
costs ... 3.16
disclosure — see (see Disclosure)
discretionary trusts ... 2.2
drafting — see (see Drafting memorandum of wishes)
economic settlors ... 7.1–7.4
exert residual influence, to ... 1.4
fiduciary considerations ... 9.2
history ... 2.1
in wills ... 8.1
language of judicial support ... 3.3
not negate fiduciary obligations owed by trustee ... 3.7
review of ... 5.5
rudimentary ... 4.7
single settlor simple option ... 11.5
subsequent or updating ... 5.3
– later wishes supersede earlier wishes ... 5.4
– settlors obliged to update ... 5.2
– weight of earlier *vs.* later wishes ... 5.1
trust documents ... 2.3
trustees, informs ... 1.5
trustees' reliance on ... 3.1–3.16
trust terms varied by ... 3.15
two settlors simple option ... 11.6

Multiple trusts ... 10.2

N

Nominee settlors
trust landscape, long-term feature of ... 7.3
variations of trust ... 7.4
wishes attributed ... 7.1

O

Ownership of wishes ... 9.5

R

Rejection, settlor's wishes ... 3.6

Retention
settlor control, of ... 1.8

Paragraph

Rudimentary
memoranda of wishes ... 4.7

S

Settlor control
retention, effect ... 1.8

Settlors
addressing true ... 7.2
alienation of property ... 1.3
cannot generally direct trustees ... 1.2
drafting memoranda of wishes ... 10.1
multiple trusts ... 10.2
obligation to update memoranda of wishes ... 5.2
single settlor simple option ... 11.5
traditional role ... 1.1
two settlors simple option ... 11.6
variations of trust ... 7.4
wishes attributed to nominee ... 7.1

Settlor's wishes
rejection ... 3.6
trustees can be influenced by ... 3.2
trustees must not blindly follow ... 3.4

Single settlor
general administration ... 11.1
memorandum ... 11.1
notes ... 11.1
simple option ... 11.5
trust formation ... 11.1

T

Trust documents
memorandum of wishes ... 2.3

Trust formation
economic settlor ... 11.3
joint settlors ... 11.2
single Settlor ... 11.1

Trustees
acting properly ... 3.5
acting reasonably ... 3.10
cannot resist disclosure due to ''obligations of confidence'' ... 4.8
consideration, memorandum of wishes ... 1.7
core documents ... 6.1
decisions in accordance with terms of trust ... 3.1; 3.9
duty of impartiality ... 3.8
independently exercise their discretion ... 3.12
influenced by settlor's wishes ... 3.2
interests of beneficiaries ... 3.8

Paragraph

memoranda of wishes 1.5; 3.11
not to follow settlor's wishes 3.4; 3.11
owe fiduciary obligations to
beneficiaries 3.7
presumption 6.2
rejection of settlor's wishes 3.6
settlor control, effect retention 1.8
settlors 1.2
settlor's wishes 1.6; 3.2

Trust information
core documents 6.4
procedure for deciding whether the
presumption applies 6.6
provision 6.5

Paragraph

trustees' decisions, reasons for 6.3
trustees, presumption 6.2

Trust landscape
nominee settlors 7.3

U

Updated memoranda of wishes
settlors obliged to 5.2

W

Wills
memorandum of wishes 8.1

Made in United States
Orlando, FL
04 November 2026

90201378R00075